Dale Earnhardt Jr.

Read all of the books in this exciting,
action-packed biography series!

Hank Aaron
Barry Bonds
Joe DiMaggio
Tim Duncan
Dale Earnhardt Jr.
Lou Gehrig
Derek Jeter
Michelle Kwan
Mickey Mantle
Jesse Owens
Ichiro Suzuki
Tiger Woods

SPORTS HEROES AND LEGENDS™

Dale Earnhardt Jr.

by Matt Doeden

Lerner Publications Company/Minneapolis

For Dad

Lerner Publications Company
A division of Lerner Publishing Group
241 First Avenue North
Minneapolis, MN 55401 U.S.A.

Website address: www.lernerbooks.com

Cover photograph:
© Sam Sharpe/CORBIS

Library of Congress Cataloging-in-Publication Data

Doeden, Matt.
    Dale Earnhardt, Jr. / by Matt Doeden.
        p.   cm. — (Sports heroes and legends)
    Includes bibliographical references and index.
    ISBN-13: 978-0-8225-3067-1 (lib. bdg. : alk. paper)
    ISBN-10: 0-8225-3067-8 (lib. bdg. : alk. paper)
    1. Earnhardt, Dale, Jr.—Juvenile literature. 2. Automobile racing drivers—United States—Biography—Juvenile literature. I. Title. II. Series.
GV1032.E18D64 2006
796.72'092—dc22   2005002922

Manufactured in the United States of America
1 2 3 4 5 6 – JR – 10 09 08 07 06 05

Contents

Daytona Champion

When Dale Earnhardt Jr. climbed into his car just before the 2004 Daytona 500, he knew that he had nothing left to prove. After growing up in the shadow of his father, NASCAR champion Dale Earnhardt, Dale Jr. had made a name for himself. In four years of full-time competition at the highest level of stock car racing, he'd demonstrated that he had the skill to succeed.

Yet Dale had never won the Daytona 500, NASCAR's biggest race. It was the first race of the 2004 Nextel Cup season, and Dale was among a small handful of drivers expected to compete for the championship. A win at Daytona would seal his place among NASCAR's best drivers and would start him on his quest to become the 2004 champion.

Dale's preparations for the race had started long before he climbed into his red-and-white No. 8 Chevrolet that Sunday afternoon. Dale and his racing team had spent months preparing and testing their car. A week earlier, Dale had run a fast qualifying time, earning a starting spot in second row. Later in the week, Greg Biffle, who had won the pole position with the fastest time, had to change his engine. By NASCAR rules, Biffle had to give up his starting position and move to the back of the pack. It was bad news for Biffle but great news for Dale, who got to move up into his spot. At a superspeedway like Daytona, starting in first place isn't that big of an advantage, but it certainly couldn't hurt.

As soon as President George W. Bush gave the drivers the starting command, Dale fired his engine and rolled his car onto Daytona's racing surface. He led forty-two other colorful stock cars around the track as the drivers warmed up their engines. When the green flag waved to signal the start of the race, Dale stepped down hard on the accelerator. The crowd roared as Dale led the pack into the first turn.

Dale stayed in front for the first twenty-nine laps of the race, but after a slow pit stop, he fell behind 2002 NASCAR champion Tony Stewart. Stewart looked like he might just have the fastest car on the track. He led almost half of the race's laps, but Dale was never far behind.

As the end of the race neared, Dale was running in second place behind Stewart. Time after time, he tried to get by

Stewart's orange No. 20 car. Finally, with about twenty laps left, Dale made a zigzag move that drivers call "pulling the pin" to pass Stewart and take the lead.

"I got a great run through [turns] three and four, knew I was going to be able to go to one side of Tony one way or the other," Dale explained. "Tony was going to block the bottom so I went to the top. He shot up in front of me at the top and I went across the back bumper of his car to the inside. . . . Once he realized I was down there, he gave me the lane."

Stewart wasn't ready to give up, though. He tried passing Dale low and high. He tried passing him in the turns and down the straightaway. But Dale's car was too fast. No matter how hard he tried, Stewart couldn't squeeze by him. Stewart understood how important drafting was at Daytona, so he decided to make the best of the situation. When drafting, cars work together to reduce wind resistance and go faster. Stewart followed very closely behind Dale. If he couldn't win, he could at least draft behind the best car and finish second.

"Dale Jr. has been the class of the field all week," Stewart said after the race. "There wasn't going to be any stopping him. It was just a matter of time. When he decided he was ready to go, he went."

No one else could challenge Dale in the final laps of the race. The crowd stood and cheered wildly as Dale crossed the

3

finish line, taking the checkered flag and his first Daytona 500 victory. The win came exactly six years after his father first won the race and three years after Dale Sr. was killed on its final lap. Dale Jr. said that as he drove, he felt like his dad was riding with him, having a blast.

Dale drove onto the grass in the middle of the track and spun in circles, celebrating his win while the crowd continued screaming. He parked his car on the finish line and hopped out the driver's side window. He waved and celebrated with his teammates as cameras flashed all around them.

"It's just the greatest race, it's the greatest day of my life," said Dale. "I can't really describe it."

Chapter One

Born to Race

When Ralph Dale Earnhardt Jr. was born on October 10, 1974, in Concord, North Carolina, he already seemed destined to become a race car driver. His father, Dale Sr., was a driver working hard to break into the big time. His grandfather, Dale Sr.'s father, Ralph, had been a famous short track driver.

RALPH EARNHARDT

Dale's grandfather had a reputation as one of the best short track drivers in the southern United States during the 1950s and 1960s. Short track drivers race on small tracks that are often unpaved. In 1956 Ralph was the Late Model Sportsman division (later called the Busch Series) champion. Ralph died of a heart attack in 1973, the year before Dale Jr. was born.

For the first several years of his life, Dale and his older sister, Kelley, lived with their parents. But after Dale Sr. and Brenda divorced in 1977, the children stayed with their mother.

By the time Dale Jr. was five years old, his father was racing full-time in NASCAR's Winston Cup series, the highest level of stock car racing in the world. Dale Sr. didn't have a lot of time at home. The racing season started in February and lasted until early November, with events at tracks all across the country. Dale and Kelley loved their father, but they missed him and wished they could see him more often.

 NASCAR stands for the National Association for Stock Car Auto Racing.

Dale Sr.'s driving career took off quickly. In 1979 he won the Winston Cup's Rookie of the Year award. The following year, he won his first championship. (Drivers earn a certain number of points based on how they finish each race, and the driver with the most points at the end of the season is the champion.) Dale Sr.'s success meant that he had plenty of money to make sure Dale and Kelley would always be well cared for. But it also meant he was busier than ever.

6

Dale Sr. remarried in 1982. That same year, bad wiring caused the house Dale and Kelley lived in with their mother to burn down. Brenda couldn't afford to build a new house for the family, so she sent the children to live with their father and new stepmother, Teresa. Brenda moved to Virginia, where her family lived.

When Dale was ten, he learned that he had an older half brother named Kerry. Before marrying Brenda, Dale Sr. had been married to a woman named Latane Key. She was Kerry's mother. Kerry was five years older than Dale.

All of this change was tough on Dale. He was a rebellious child, often acting out and behaving badly. He had little respect for authority and often got in trouble at school. Dale Sr. worried about his youngest son. When Dale was in seventh grade, his father sent him to the Oak Ridge Military Academy in Greensboro, North Carolina. Life changed drastically for Dale. The teachers at Oak Ridge were strict and didn't tolerate bad behavior. Dale quickly learned to dress neatly, act courteously, and show respect for authority. He stayed at Oak Ridge for the rest of seventh grade and all of eighth grade.

While Dale's behavior improved, he still desperately wanted his father's attention. Dale Sr. was becoming one of the biggest stars in racing, and the demands on his time grew with every year. When he wasn't getting ready for a race, he was dealing with car sponsors or the media. He also had his own business, a

Chevrolet dealership in Newton, North Carolina, to worry about.

"Dale Jr. played soccer . . . but Dad never got to be a part of that," Kelley said. "We told him about what we did and he congratulated us, but it wasn't the same as him being there."

Still, Dale Sr. had a huge influence on his son. When his father raced in nearby Charlotte, North Carolina, Dale Jr. could see the races in person. Other races were broadcast on television. Dale watched his dad win thrilling races and Winston Cup championships.

THE INTIMIDATOR

Dale Earnhardt Sr. earned the nickname "The Intimidator" on the racetrack. He was willing to do whatever it took to win, including spinning out an opponent to make a pass. Other NASCAR drivers quickly learned to fear and respect Earnhardt's black No. 3 car.

From an early age, Dale was fascinated with cars. As a child, he'd cut pictures of cars out of magazines and pretended to race them on a table. His interest only grew as he got older.

"I wasn't really into working on the cars or knowing or learning about the cars," Dale said. "I was just really interested in what it was like being a driver and the things you had to do."

When Dale was thirteen, he finally met his older half brother, who was already eighteen. Despite the age difference, Dale and Kerry quickly became friends. They shared a love of cars and racing, and Dale was happy to finally have his brother in his life.

Kart Racing

When Dale was thirteen, his dad bought him a go-kart. Go-karts are small, gas-powered four-wheel racers. Dale loved driving the kart, but he didn't drive it safely. Soon Dale Sr. decided that the kart was too dangerous and took it away.

Dale's desire to become a driver was growing. He had to wait three more years before he could get a license to drive, and the wait was killing him. He begged his dad to help him race earlier, but Dale Sr. told him he had to be patient. In the meantime, he attended nearby Mooresville High School.

When Dale was finally able to drive, there was no stopping him. At age seventeen, he bought a red Chevrolet Monte Carlo. He worked on the engine and tried to make the car as fast as he could. He started his racing career in that car, driving it at Concord Motorsport Park.

Dale graduated from high school in 1992. As long as he could remember, his father had stressed the importance of education. Because of this, Dale was bitterly disappointed when his father was unable to attend his graduation because of a race.

After high school, Dale enrolled at Mitchell Community College, a local trade school, to study automotive repair. But racing remained his goal in life. He went to a driving school run by Andy Hillenburg. There he learned advanced racing strategies and techniques. All the teachers and students at the school knew who Dale was, or at least who his father was. Dale realized that he would never be just another driver. No matter what he did, he would always be the son of Dale Earnhardt, the man whom many people felt was best stock car driver in the world.

Dale knew he had to find a way to live up to the expectations that came with the name Earnhardt. "You could tell that if he didn't have the experience, he was going to get it," Hillenburg said of his young student. "If he didn't have the talent, he was going to figure it out and get the talent. There was a lot of determination on his part."

Determination wasn't enough to pay the bills, though. When Dale came home with a speeding ticket one day, his father told him that he had to get a job to pay the fine. Dale's first job was at a gas station. He later started work at his father's car dealership, where he did oil changes and worked on engine and auto body repairs. Although he enjoyed the work, he often found himself thinking about racing.

❝Anybody who was around when I was a kid knows that Dad never handed me a thing. He was real careful about that.❞

—DALE EARNHARDT JR.

Dale Sr. was determined that his son would earn his own way into a racing career. His father, Ralph, had treated him the same way. He felt it was important that Dale learn what he needed to know on his own.

Dale wasn't alone as he tried to follow in his father's footsteps. Kerry had also decided that he wanted to be a driver. The brothers talked nonstop about cars and racing. Together they dreamed about what they might accomplish in NASCAR's biggest races.

Chapter | Two

Track Training

While Dale continued attending trade school, he became more serious about racing. In 1992 he drove a "Legends" car at nearby Charlotte Motor Speedway, one of the tracks his father drove on during the Winston Cup season. Legends cars are small replicas of old cars. In October Dale scored his first win at Charlotte. On the last lap of the race he caught race leader Hank Jones, who owned the car Dale was driving. Dale bumped Jones to make the winning pass. The race showed that Dale was willing to do whatever it took to win, even trade paint with a friend.

Dale joined a race team full-time in 1993. Gary Hargett owned a car that ran in the Saturday night late-model series at Myrtle Beach Speedway in South Carolina. Late-model cars are a type of light stock car that must fit a rigid set of rules about the engine and body shape. Hargett was an old family friend, having worked with both Ralph and Dale Sr. He thought Dale Jr. showed a lot of raw talent, and he wanted the chance to help him become a better racer. Hargett spent weeks convincing Dale Sr. to let his youngest son drive the car. Dale Sr. suggested that maybe Kerry was the driver Hargett wanted, but Hargett stood firm. He wanted Dale Jr.

Dale's name certainly helped to open some doors in his career, but it also made him a target. Many of his fellow racers didn't respect him. They thought he was just driving on his father's name. On the track, many were eager to take out the son of NASCAR's best driver.

Dale's looks also made him a target. He was small and thin and had a very young-looking face. Some people thought he looked too young to be driving. Many drivers thought they could take advantage of the baby-faced driver.

Dale often felt frustrated by the treatment the other drivers gave him on the track. Hargett told him to be patient. Many of the drivers he raced against dreamed of beating a NASCAR champion like Dale Earnhardt Sr. But they'd never be able to do that. Beating his son was close enough. It was the price he had to pay for being named Earnhardt.

"The first year we ran down there, everybody wanted to [spin] Junior around," Hargett commented. "They roughed him up bad that first year."

Dale quickly learned that the best way to stop the harsh treatment on the track was to fight back. During one race, he was leading on the final lap when another driver spun him out. He knew he had to prove that he wouldn't just sit back and take it. The next time Dale was on the track with the driver, he spun him into a steel gate on the first lap. It was a violent crash and the other drivers took notice. Dale's message got through, and his problems on the track quickly disappeared. Suddenly the other drivers treated him with respect, just like any other driver. Track officials often penalize this type of driving. But still, many drivers believe it's important that the other drivers on the track know that they're willing to break the rules to protect themselves.

Dale's wild driving style often worried Hargett. Dale stomped down on the gas pedal and always tried to run at full speed. After years of watching his father's aggressive style, it was the only way he knew how to drive. He wasn't afraid to bump into another driver if it gave him a chance to make a pass.

While Dale ran races at Myrtle Beach, Kerry was trying to make a name for himself at nearby Hickory Motor Speedway. Even Kelley had decided to give racing a try. Unlike many other sports, women compete head-to-head with men in auto racing. She drove at Caraway Speedway in Asheboro, North Carolina. Kelley later decided that racing wasn't for her, but Dale and Kerry kept at their dream.

DARRELL WALTRIP

Dale may have had one of the most famous drivers of all time as a father, but Dale Sr. wasn't the only driver he looked up to. Darrell Waltrip was another of Dale's favorites. Waltrip won three NASCAR titles in the early 1980s and was one of Dale Sr.'s biggest rivals on the track. His younger brother, Michael Waltrip, followed in his footsteps and made his Winston Cup debut in 1985.

On August 20, 1994, Dale won his first late-model feature race at Myrtle Beach. He celebrated the win with his friends and teammates, but many people downplayed the victory. The best late-model drivers at Myrtle Beach, Charles Powell, Robert Powell, and their half brother, Sean Graham, weren't driving in that race. People told Dale that until he beat the Powell brothers, he hadn't won anything.

Dale didn't win at all in 1995. The Powell brothers were too dominant. Although Dale might not have been able to beat the track favorites, he learned from them. He watched how they approached each turn and how they drove differently during a race's final laps. In time, Dale formed a friendship with Robert Powell.

"Everybody is always trying to ride him and all," Powell said. "I just took him as Dale Jr. . . . . He knew I didn't look at him as a rich kid or whatever, because I knew he struggled and had to earn what he got."

During his three years driving at Myrtle Beach, Dale lived for racing. He often stayed at the Hargett home so he could be near the race shop. He worked on the car whenever he could. As time went on, people began to recognize the young driver. Dale found himself signing autographs and getting his picture taken with fans. For the first time in his life, people were starting to notice him for his own achievements rather than just as the son of a famous driver.

By 1996 twenty-one-year-old Dale Earnhardt Jr. was ready to make a change. He left Hargett's racing team and joined a team based out of his father's nearby shop. He drove late models at Myrtle Beach and several other tracks in the area.

Dale was enjoying success but was still having a hard time winning consistently. He ran sixteen races at a track in Florence, South Carolina, and finished in second place fourteen times. He won once and had an engine failure the other time. Finishing near the front almost all of the time was a mark of a good driver, but Dale was eager to show that he was a winner.

RACING FLAGS

NASCAR officials use a system of flags to communicate with drivers. A flagman sits high above the start/finish line and waves a flag to signal the race condition.

Green flag: Waved to start a race and to restart a race after a caution

Yellow flag: Waved to signal a caution to drivers

Red flag: Waved to stop all of the cars—the track is unsafe to drive

Black flag: Waved to signal a penalty for an individual driver

White flag: Waved to signal the final lap

Checkered flag: Waved to signal the end of the race

On June 22, 1996, he got the perfect chance to prove that he had the skill to drive at a higher level. NASCAR's Busch

Series came to Myrtle Beach for the Carolina Pride 250. The Busch Series is NASCAR's second level of stock car racing. It is a training ground for drivers who want to prepare for NASCAR's highest level of stock car racing. Driving in a Busch Series race would be a huge step in Dale's quest to follow in his father's footsteps.

Dale prepared to make a qualifying run for the race. He knew he had an advantage over many of the other drivers—Myrtle Beach had been his home track for three years. He knew it better than almost everyone else in the field.

Dale's hard work and knowledge of the track paid off. He qualified in seventh position for the race, an impressive start for a driver in his first Busch race. His experience on the track helped, but he quickly learned that he was in for a whole new kind of race. Busch cars are heavier and more powerful than late models. They handle differently. This forced Dale to adjust the line he took around the track. He had to enter and exit turns differently. He had to learn to handle the more powerful car on the track he knew so well.

"You have to run a totally different line with the Busch cars," he said. "The late models can go through the corners a little bit easier. The Busch cars are totally different. They have a lot more weight and horsepower."

Dale ran well during the race, but an early spin followed by a mistake in the pits put him a lap down and cost him the chance to win. Because he was a lap down and not competing for Busch Series points, he had to start near the back at every restart (the field of cars restarts the race together after every caution flag), making it almost impossible for him to earn his lap back. But even from the back of the pack, he put on a performance far more impressive than his fourteenth-place finish indicated.

 Dale's fourteenth place finish in his first Busch race earned him $1,880.

"We passed cars all race long," he said. "I stayed in the back, out of everybody's way. Then I'd pass 'em again. It was like we passed everyone there, over and over."

Dale had given stock car racing fans a glimpse of what was to come. It was time for him to begin building that future.

Chapter Three

Busch Series Star

Dale's strong showing at the Carolina Pride 250 attracted the attention of fans and fellow drivers. It also got the attention of Dale Earnhardt Sr., who was impressed with his son's performance. In 1997 Dale Sr. asked Dale Jr. if he wanted to drive a Busch car for his own racing team, Dale Earnhardt Incorporated (DEI). Dale wasted little time in accepting the offer. He would run a partial schedule in 1997, preparing to run a full season in 1998. The new deal also gave Dale a chance to spend more time with his father. Busch events are often held at the same track and on the same weekend as Winston Cup events. Dale Jr. would be racing on Saturday while his father raced on Sunday.

Dale's first Busch start of 1997 came in April at the BellSouth Mobility/Opryland 320 at the Nashville Speedway in Tennessee. He qualified in nineteenth place for the race, but engine trouble left him with a disappointing thirty-ninth-place finish. He finished only 93 of the 320 laps.

Dale hoped for better luck in his next start, at the Lysol 200 at Watkins Glen, New York, a road course. Many young drivers have troubles at road courses. Their many twists and turns present a different challenge from oval tracks. A new track didn't change Dale's luck, though. Again equipment problems knocked him out of the race early and left him with another thirty-ninth-place finish. His bad luck continued at the Gateway 300, where a wreck dropped him to thirty-eighth place.

QUALIFYING

A driver's first job is to qualify for each race. To qualify, each driver runs two laps alone on the track. The faster of these two laps becomes the driver's qualifying time. The driver with the fastest time starts first, in the pole position. The second-fastest driver starts alongside the fastest driver, on the outside part of the track. This position is called the "outside pole." The rest of the drivers line up behind these two cars according to their qualifying times.

The year 1997 was supposed to be Dale's time to learn what it takes to drive stock cars in NASCAR's "minor league."

Nobody expected him to be an instant success. But still, the terrible start caused him to question his confidence. Since he had started racing, fans and other drivers had wondered whether the youngster really belonged. Suddenly Dale was wondering the same thing himself.

On August 16 at the Detroit Gasket 200 in Michigan, Dale's luck finally changed. After qualifying eighteenth, Dale drove a great race. He finished in seventh place and got a much-needed confidence boost.

Dale's success carried into qualifying the next week, where he earned the outside pole, or second starting position, at the Food City 250 at Bristol Motor Speedway. The race didn't go as well as qualifying, though. Dale quickly fell back in the pack and was lapped. By the race's end, he had fallen three laps down. He crossed the finish line in twenty-second place, a real disappointment after an excellent qualifying run.

Dale ran three more races in 1997, finishing thirty-fourth, sixteenth, and thirteenth. The steady improvement gave his father and teammates confidence. Dale was ready to run a full schedule of Busch races.

Dale and his DEI teammates entered the 1998 Busch Series full of high hopes and expectations. DEI was becoming more and more established in stock car racing, with teams at every major level of the sport. Dale was stepping into a car that Steve

Park had driven the year before. Park's season had been so successful that DEI had moved him up to the Winston Cup. Dale's crew chief was Tony Eury Sr., a longtime friend of his father. As crew chief, Eury's job was to oversee the entire race team. He decided which changes to make to the car. During the race, Eury talked with Dale over the radio. Together they made the team's strategy decisions.

"All the ingredients were there to run well," Dale later noted. "We just had to find out whether I could do it."

NASCAR TRACKS

NASCAR races are held on a variety of tracks. Most are ovals, but even the ovals come in many different types. Talladega Superspeedway, the biggest oval, is more than 2.6 miles around. But Bristol Motor Speedway is only half a mile around. Road courses like Watkins Glen International aren't ovals at all. They have many twists and turns.

Everything looked great for Dale and his team as they qualified for the first race of the season, the NAPA Auto Parts 300 at Daytona, Florida. Dale rolled the No. 3 Chevrolet, sponsored by ACDelco, onto the track for his qualifying run. He stomped on the accelerator and ran a great qualifying lap, earning the third starting spot for the race. Dale was comfortable racing at Daytona, where teams must add restrictor plates to their engines to limit horsepower and speed. Restrictor plates are added to cars at very large oval tracks because without them, the cars can reach speeds that are dangerous to both drivers and spectators. The good lap gave Dale a great starting spot. The year was starting off right.

All the good feelings Dale and his team had entering the NAPA 300 quickly disappeared, though. After staying in the top five for the early laps of the race, Dale came in for his first pit stop. He didn't slow down quickly enough as he approached his pit box, where his pit crew was ready to change his tires and add fuel to the car. The team's jack man had to jump out of the way to avoid being run over. Dale's car slid over the line that marks the pit box. A team cannot work on a car that isn't completely inside the pit box. Dale had to quickly shift into reverse to back up. But he didn't shift cleanly, and as he tried to back up, he broke the car's drive shaft.

The mistake ended Dale's chances of winning. The team had to repair the car. It sat still in the garage while all the other cars sped around the track. By the time the repairs were done, Dale had fallen almost twenty laps behind the leaders.

Still, Dale knew that he was a full-time Busch driver. He was competing for a season championship, and every lap mattered.

Even though he had no chance of winning, he had to go back onto the track to earn every spot—and every point—he could.

Dale didn't go back out onto the track looking for anything big. He just wanted to keep turning laps and stay out of trouble. But trouble found him on the 105th lap when Dick Trickle accidentally tapped him from behind on the backstretch. Dale's car lifted into the air and flipped over before smashing back down onto Trickle's car.

❝*I hate watching a race that looks like a bunch of toy soldiers marching around. Fans like action, even if their favorite driver gets bumped around or spun out.*❞

—DALE EARNHARDT JR.

"Somebody hit me in the right rear," Trickle said of the accident. "It got my car turned sideways and that started it all. It wasn't Dale Jr.'s fault. He showed he belongs out there. I never had any doubt. I thought, 'Well, at least he got a soft landing, because he landed on my windshield and hood.'"

Dale got bounced around and bruised in the crash, and his car was wrecked, but neither he nor Trickle suffered any major injuries. He was okay, but his season had started terribly. It was not the way he had hoped to begin his career as a full-time Busch Series driver.

Dale was determined not to let the disappointing finish get him down. Two weeks later, at the Sam's Town 300 in Las Vegas, he had his best race yet. After staying near the front for most of the race, Dale worked his way through the field to second place. Jimmy Spencer, who had been leading for much of the race, was the only man between Dale and his first win.

With only eleven laps left, a five-car accident brought out a caution flag. NASCAR officials stopped the race to clean up the mess. The caution set up a ten-lap sprint to the finish.

Dale knew that Spencer had been having trouble with restarts all day. If Dale could get a good restart, he had a good chance to take the lead. But instead, he timed the green flag poorly and found himself fighting off the third-place car of Joe Nemechek. Four laps later, Nemechek passed Dale. Dale took second place back with only four laps remaining. He knew he had to hurry if he was going to catch Spencer. Slowly Dale closed in. As Spencer crossed the start/finish line with one lap to go, he slowed down, forcing Dale to do the same. Spencer quickly sped back up and widened his lead. Dale wasn't able to catch him again.

"It seemed like we had the car to beat," Dale said. "But a little inexperience as a driver cost me."

Dale was disappointed that he couldn't get his first win, but he was also happy. The second-place finish was by far his best as a Busch driver.

A month later, Dale won his first pole at Bristol Motor Speedway. He finished the race in second place, about ten car lengths behind winner Elliott Sadler. The following week, Dale and his teammates headed to Texas Motor Speedway for the Coca-Cola 300. While second-place finishes were good, Dale was ready for a win.

Dale started the race in sixteenth place but showed early that he had a strong car. He slowly climbed through the field. Finally, with about twenty laps left, he was in the lead. But Dale knew that he couldn't just cruise to a win. He still had to make one more pit stop. His team had a big decision to make. Should he take four new tires or should he save time in the pits by taking only two tires?

Dale made the decision. He needed the grip four new tires would give him. He exited pit row in third place with only eleven laps remaining. Dale quickly made up one of the spots he'd lost on pit row. He was chasing the leader, Joe Nemechek, when an accident brought out a caution flag.

The caution set up a restart with only five laps left. Drivers often call a restart with only a few laps left a "shoot-out." Dale tried to make the pass for the lead, but Nemechek kept holding on. With only two laps left, Dale was getting impatient. He didn't want to finish second again. He wanted to win. So Dale borrowed one of his father's strategies. He drove his Chevrolet right up behind Nemechek, pushing his nose right up to the leader's bumper. The move was designed to make Nemechek's car get loose, or lose grip. It worked. Nemechek moved up the track slightly. It was a small move, but it was enough. Dale dove to the bottom of the track and made the pass. A lap later, he crossed the finish line with his first Busch Series win.

"I haven't raised [Dale] to be like me. I tried to raise him to be his own person.**"**

—DALE EARNHARDT SR.

The crowd erupted with cheers. Dale's teammates celebrated from the pits. Even Dale Earnhardt Sr., known for being tough and emotionless, had tears in his eyes as he joined his son in Victory Lane. All the hard work had finally paid off. Dale Earnhardt Jr. was no longer a second-place driver. He was a winner.

After Dale got out of his car, he hugged his father. Later he was asked if the hug was an emotional moment for him. Dale said, "The most emotional of my life. It stirred memories of the years I tried so hard to earn my dad's approval. Maybe that did it." The win was the highlight of Dale's young career. He had shown that even as a rookie, he could drive with the best. Nobody knew then just how much the rookie could achieve.

Chapter | Four

A Rookie, a Champion

Dale's win at Texas came in the seventh race of 1998, less than a quarter of the way through the Busch Series season. At the time, few people considered the twenty-three-year-old to be a real contender for the Busch Series championship. Many thought he was too young and too inexperienced. Some still dismissed him as being just the son of a famous driver, good enough to win a race now and then, but certainly not talented enough to compete for a championship.

For a while, those doubters appeared to be right. After following up his win with an eighth-place finish at Hickory Motor Speedway, Dale's team went through a rough stretch, wrecking in three out of four races at one point. The team dropped farther and farther down the standings each week, and frustration grew. But while Dale was discouraged, he wasn't ready to give up on the season.

By the end of May, Dale badly needed a strong finish. He started sixteenth in the MBNA 200 at Dover International Speedway, the same starting spot he'd held for his first win two months earlier. Dale dominated the field and won easily despite an early spinout. Good pit strategy and a strong car were enough for an impressive four-second win over Bobby Hillin. For the second time, Dale stood in victory lane with his teammates, hoisting the winner's trophy over his head. He also held a new track record for average speed—130.152 miles per hour—breaking the old record by more than 3.5 miles per hour.

To win a championship, a team needs consistent finishes. So far, Dale's season had been very up and down—he seemed to finish either near the front or at the back. Winning races wasn't going to be enough. Dale had to find a way to finish near the front every week. Because NASCAR's points system rewards drivers for consistency, finishing fifth two races in a row is better than winning one week and finishing fortieth the next.

The win at Dover seemed to change everything. Dale scored top-ten finishes in each of the next six races, an impressive accomplishment for any driver, especially a rookie. Dale Sr. was also impressed. He finally believed that his son was going to be a NASCAR star. On June 12, DEI signed Dale Jr. to a five-year contract. Dale was happy to have a job for the next five years—few young drivers have such security because most team owners won't commit millions of dollars in equipment to inexperienced drivers. He was even happier that he would be driving for his father.

Dale's next win came at the DieHard 250 in Milwaukee, Wisconsin, on July 5. After starting second, Dale dominated, leading 208 of the race's 250 laps. At one point in the race, he held an amazing twenty-eight-second lead and almost lapped the entire field. It was the easiest win of Dale's career.

"We were just awesome," he said. "Tony Eury Sr. and Tony Eury Jr. told me this car was going to be awesome today. They were right."

Dale wasted little time proving that his father's trust was well placed. On July 19, he won the Kenwood Home & Car Auto 300 at California Speedway. It was another dominating performance. After starting the race second, Dale took the lead from Robert Pressley on the first lap. He led all but nine of the 150 laps for his fourth win of the year. Dale was excited about the win, but he was even more excited about the Busch Series points standings. The win moved him into first place, six points ahead of Matt Kenseth.

TONY EURY SR.

Beginning in 1998, Dale's crew chief was Tony Eury Sr. Eury started his racing career as a driver. Dale's grandfather, Ralph, built some of his engines. Soon Eury began working with Dale Sr. By 1985 Eury was working full-time for DEI. His son, Tony Jr., is Dale's age and also became part of the DEI team.

"We're going for the championship and that has been our focus all along," Dale said after the race. "Winning races is a great bonus, but the championship is the main focus."

Dale had more than just the points lead. He had also become the most popular driver in the Busch Series. The fans loved him. The media constantly wanted interviews. Dale had seen his father handle pressure and popularity, so he was not as shocked as other rookie drivers might have been in his place. But still, the constant demand for his attention was a distraction.

The next week, Dale was looking to continue his hot streak. He won the pole for the Lycos.com 300 at South Boston

Speedway, but NASCAR penalized him for rough driving during the race. He finished thirteenth but held his points lead because Kenseth finished only one spot ahead of him. Still, Dale knew that he couldn't afford to give Kenseth any more chances. His dad had a reputation as a rough driver and Dale didn't want to start earning the same reputation. He wanted to follow his own style.

Dale's crew chief, Tony Eury Sr., didn't mind his young driver's aggressive style. "Dale Jr. gets a little wild sometimes on the racetrack, and we've got to calm him down," he said. "But it's a lot easier to get that attitude out of a driver than it is to put it in one."

Dale quickly made up for his mistake at South Boston by winning the Kroger NASCAR 200 in Indianapolis, Indiana. He started the race sixteenth and quickly moved up through the field. He passed Elliott Sadler for the lead a little past the halfway mark of the race. Once he had the lead, Dale never looked back, cruising to his fifth win of the year.

A month later came one of the most exciting races of the season. After a poor qualifying run, Dale started thirty-fourth in the Dura Lube 200 at Darlington Raceway. But the bad starting position didn't get him down. He charged through the field and was in the top ten when an accident brought out a caution flag. During the caution, the team had to make a decision. Should Dale come in for a pit stop and fresh tires? He would give up a few spots on the track if he did. But the team didn't think he would be able to pass the leaders on old tires. They decided to take a chance and have him come in for a stop.

The race restarted with twelve laps to go. Dale's fresh tires allowed him to quickly move through the field. He passed Mike McLaughlin, Mark Martin, and Dale Jarrett to take second place. He was charging hard toward race leader Dick Trickle when another caution flag flew. According to NASCAR rules, there weren't enough laps left to restart the race, so the race was over. Trickle had won by only four inches. If the caution flag hadn't come, Dale almost certainly would have won.

Dale and his teammates would have liked another win, but they weren't too disappointed. A second-place finish was great for the points standings.

66*[Dad] has done so much for me in racing and life. I feel compelled to drive for him and try to win as many races and championships as I can, to try to pay him back.*99

—DALE EARNHARDT JR.

Racing for points was important, but Dale also wanted to win. His next chance came a week later at the Autolite Platinum

250 in Richmond, Virginia. After qualifying second, Dale turned in another strong performance. He led all but fourteen of the 250 laps in winning his sixth race of the year. More important, Dale increased his lead in the standings to 140 points. With only six races left in the season, Dale was moving closer and closer to his goal—a Busch Series championship.

Kenseth wasn't going to go away easily, though. He won the next race while Dale finished eighth, trimming the lead to 107 points. In the following race, Kenseth finished second while Dale finished third. With four races left, Dale's lead was down to 102 points. It was still a nice lead, but one bad race could wipe it away completely. Dale wanted a bigger cushion.

On October 17, a week after Dale's twenty-fourth birthday, the drivers were in Madison, Illinois, for the Carquest Auto Parts 250. Dale started the race in thirteenth place. Kenseth started in tenth. Both drivers had strong cars and quickly moved to the front, each taking the lead for a while. On the last pit stop, Dale's pit made a few adjustments that improved the car and allowed him to drive to the win. Even though Kenseth finished second, it was still a good day for Dale in the standings. Dale had gained only five points, but time was running out for Kenseth.

"We're far enough behind at this point that we can't go out and win it," Kenseth said. "[Dale] can do something to lose it, but we can't win it on our own."

Dale and his teammates knew what Kenseth meant. As long as Dale didn't find any trouble in the last three races, he would win the title. The only way he could lose it would be to have a bad race, a crash, or blow up an engine.

Dale didn't make any big mistakes in the next two races, finishing fourteenth and second. He finished ahead of Kenseth in both races and all but locked up the championship. In the last race, the Jiffy Lube Miami 300, he needed only to start the race to win the title. There was no way Dale was going to miss the race. "I'll climb in my car next week if my legs and all my bones are broken," he boasted.

Dale was joking, but he also meant what he said. That week, Dale didn't take any chances. He stayed indoors. He didn't go anywhere or do anything that could hurt him. When he finally got into his car and completed the first lap of the season's final race on November 14, the championship chase was officially over. It was a good thing he'd built a big lead, too, because his engine blew up about halfway through the race and he finished forty-second.

It didn't matter, though. Dale won the championship by 48 points. It was an amazing year for a rookie. Before the season, nobody expected him to win seven races and a NASCAR title.

"I got to win this championship with a lot of special people," Dale said after the race. "My dad, Tony Eury, my crew chief, and Tony Jr. I had no idea what to expect or how to win a championship. . . . We're going to have a good time when we get back [home]."

Dale and his teammates celebrated their accomplishment, but they didn't lose sight of their long-term goals. Another big step lay ahead in 1999.

Chapter Five

Trying to Repeat

Dale's amazing rookie year didn't go unnoticed by the racing world. In September the Budweiser company offered Dale a six-year sponsorship contract for a Winston Cup car. It was an amazing offer from one of the richest sponsors in the sport. And they were asking Dale, a driver who had never even run in a Winston Cup race. Signing with such a big sponsor would mean Dale and his DEI team would always have a good chance to compete. Because stock car racing is so expensive, teams need money from sponsors to build a good car. The richer the sponsor, the more money the team can put into developing their cars. The Budweiser deal would ensure that Dale always had great equipment and a great team behind him.

Dale discussed the contract with his dad and other DEI team members. They quickly agreed to accept. According to the deal, Dale would continue to drive full-time on the Busch Series. His main goal of 1999 would be to defend his championship. But he would also take part in a few Winston Cup races, where he would drive the number 8 Bud car. Dale was in for a busy year.

"For someone to take a chance on a young driver like me means so much," Dale said. "Everybody's taking a risk here. That's obvious. But I think I'm capable of doing what they want."

RIDING IN STYLE

When DEI and Budweiser announced their new six-year sponsorship deal, it wasn't just an ordinary press conference. Dale rode into the conference on a wagon that was pulled by eight Clydesdale horses, a longtime symbol of the company that makes Budweiser.

Dale's career was finally taking shape. While he enjoyed his Busch Series title, he looked forward to bigger things. He hadn't dreamed all his life of winning a championship in NASCAR's second level of stock car racing. He'd imagined racing against his father for the Winston Cup title. To him, the Busch Series was only a stepping-stone, a place to gain experience and show that he belonged.

Dale didn't have to wait until 1999 to race his dad, though. In November 1998, father and son traveled with other drivers to Japan for an exhibition race. For most drivers, the race wasn't important. It didn't count as an official NASCAR race. Nobody earned championship points or a big check. But it was a big deal for Dale. He was going to race against his father. He later said that he was more excited about that than he had been about winning the Busch Series title a month earlier. Dale didn't win the exhibition race in Japan, but he did accomplish his goal—he beat his dad. Dale Jr. finished sixth and Dale Sr. ended up eighth.

❝ *It felt good to beat my dad in Japan because he didn't think I could do it. He always doesn't think I can do it and I like to prove it to him. When you do succeed, he still says 'I could have done it better.'* ❞

—DALE EARNHARDT JR.

Everything seemed to be going Dale's way. He headed for the first race of the Busch season in February feeling like he was on top of the world. But the opening week quickly brought him back to reality. First, he crashed his car in the International Race of Champions (IROC) event at Daytona. (IROC events include drivers from many different types of racing. In addition to NASCAR drivers, Indy car drivers, Formula One drivers, and others take part.) Next, he crashed his main car during a practice session before the NAPA Auto Parts 300. He had to enter the race in a backup car, which he also crashed.

Dale's Busch season hadn't started well, but after qualifying for the pole in the second race, things seemed to be improving. His bad start took a turn for the worse, however, when, for the second race in a row, Dale crashed. He finished in thirty-fifth place. His defense of his title was not going well.

It wasn't a good way to begin the season, but it was only two races. Dale turned his season around, finishing in the top ten in seven of the next eight races. He wasn't scoring wins, but he was always near the front and was moving his way back up the standings.

 The Coca-Cola 600 is the longest race in the Winston Cup.

Dale was focused on winning another Busch title, but he was also eager to make his Winston Cup debut. The Coca-Cola 600 took place in Charlotte at Lowe's Motor Speedway on

May 30. That weekend, Dale would be doing "double duty," which meant he would drive in the Busch race on Saturday and then the Winston Cup race on Sunday.

Busch series racing and Winston Cup series racing are very similar. Winston Cup cars are a bit heavier and have slightly more horsepower and speed. But the biggest difference between the two series is the length of the races. Dale's first Winston Cup race would be 600 miles long, twice as long as he was used to running in the Busch series.

Dale started the weekend well, finishing second to Mark Martin in the Carquest Auto Parts 300. Then came his big day—his Winston Cup debut. Dale felt a lot of pressure for the race. The media coverage was intense. Many people were calling the race "E Day." The fans were excited to see father and son battle on the track.

Retired NASCAR driver Ned Jarrett was amazed by the coverage of the event. "I don't remember anyone coming in who's gotten this much attention," he said. "It's unusual, to say the least. We might not ever see it again."

A good qualifying run put Dale in the eighth starting position. He fell back early, then really hurt his chances as he came in for his first pit stop. As he drove down pit road, Dale couldn't find his pit stall. He slowed down way too soon as he frantically looked for his team. By the time he found the right stall, he had lost a lot of time. The mistake wasn't entirely Dale's, though. His spotter, the team member that helps tell the driver where to go, didn't give him the right information as he entered the pits.

Shortly after the pit row mistake, race leader Jeff Burton lapped Dale, who was never able to make up that lap. By the end of the race, Dale was three laps down. He finished in sixteenth place. It wasn't the start Dale had hoped for, but at least he had finished the race. Dale Sr., meanwhile, finished sixth.

With the excitement of his Winston Cup debut behind him, Dale returned his focus the next week to his Busch team. He was second in the points chase, but he still hadn't won a race. He changed that at the MBNA Platinum 200 in Dover, where he won after starting fifteenth. The win gave him the lead in the championship standings over his familiar rival Matt Kenseth.

❝People think I'm crazy to say this, but my biggest deal is I want to stay normal while living a very abnormal life. . . . I want to do all this crazy stuff and then be able to just be a regular person in the end.❞

—DALE EARNHARDT JR.

Dale's week only got better. On June 11, he got another chance to race against his dad, this time in an IROC race. In

43

their past races, they'd been on the track at the same time, but father and son hadn't done much racing against each other. This time, they drove to the end in a battle for the win. On the final turn of the race, Dale Jr. was driving on the outside part of the track with Dale Sr. right below him on the inside. They bumped and banged to a thrilling side-by-side finish, with Dale Jr. winning by less than two feet.

"I guess you couldn't write a better script," Dale Jr. said. "I was trying with all of my might to win that race."

On June 12, Dale returned to his Busch team for the race at South Boston Speedway. The team had needed almost five months to win their first race of the 1999 season. The wait for the second win wasn't nearly as long. After a crash-filled race, Dale battled Jeff Green down the stretch. He held Green off and took the checkered flag for his second Busch Series win in a row. More important, he extended his lead over Kenseth to 64 points.

Dale was hitting his peak. The next Busch race was the Lysol 200 at Watkins Glen, a road course. Dale was charging through the field when, with twenty laps left, he began having troubles with his shifter. The car wouldn't stay in second or fourth gear. Dale had to hold on to the shifting lever to keep it from popping into another gear. Instead of steering through the demanding road course with two hands, Dale had to finish the race using just one hand.

It was a setback, but Dale didn't let it stop him. He made the adjustment and continued his charge through the field. Soon only leader Ron Fellows stood between Dale and a third straight win. But Fellows, a road course specialist, had a very strong car. It didn't look like anybody could catch him. Then, on the last lap, he had engine problems. Dale quickly took advantage.

Fellows's engine gave him the most trouble on the straightest part of the track. He couldn't reach top speed. Dale quickly closed the gap and made the pass. But when Dale had to slow down for a turn, his car popped out of gear again. Fellows caught him and drove into his bumper, trying to push him out of the way to make a pass. Dale held on and sped through the turn. Fellows couldn't catch up again and Dale crossed the finish line with his third straight win.

"It's hard enough to drive around this place with two hands," Dale said. "With one hand, that's real hard."

Dale had handled a tough situation like a seasoned veteran. Almost any good driver can win if his car is perfect. It takes a great driver to win when things aren't going quite right.

Dale's drive to a second Busch Series title was well under way. He won the Gateway 250 in July, then scored his fifth win of the year a month later in the NAPA 200 at Michigan International Speedway.

The NAPA 200 win was special to Dale because of Jeff Gordon, the driver he had to beat. Gordon, who by this time had surpassed Dale Sr. as NASCAR's best driver, was making a rare Busch Series appearance. Unlike many drivers who made occasional Busch appearances, Gordon spent almost all of his time concentrating on his Winston Cup team. Dale and Gordon had the strongest cars in the race, and soon they were alone in front, trading the lead back and forth. In the race's final laps, Dale was able to put a lapped car between himself and Gordon. Gordon couldn't get around the car in time, and Dale held on for the win.

After the race, Gordon praised the second-year driver. "Dale Jr. just beat us. That's all there is to it."

Dale scored one more victory in September at the Autolite Platinum 250 in Richmond. The win gave him a commanding lead in the standings, and he was able to clinch his second championship with a race to spare.

In two years, Dale had won thirteen races and two championships. He was ready for the next level. It was time to join his father as a Winston Cup driver.

Chapter | Six

Winston Cup Rookie

Dale had snatched a title away from Matt Kenseth two years in a row. In 2000 both drivers moved to racing in the Winston Cup full time. Neither of them was expected to have a shot at the Winston Cup championship. The other, more experienced drivers on the circuit were just too good. Instead, the rivals would spend the year battling for the Winston Cup's Rookie of the Year Award.

Twenty-four-year-old Dale Earnhardt Jr. entered the Winston Cup in a way no other rookie ever had. Most first-year drivers have low expectations and few real fans. Over time, they earn a reputation on the track and win fans. For most rookies, driving full-time in NASCAR's highest level of racing is enough pressure. But for Dale, everything was different. No rookie had ever come into the Winston Cup with the amount of attention and pressure Dale faced. "You feel like everybody's looking at you," Dale admitted. "You feel like all eyes are on you."

One example of the different kind of pressure Dale faced was many fans' desire to see him beat Jeff Gordon. Gordon had burst onto the Winston Cup scene in the early 1990s and proceeded to dominate the sport. Within a few years, Gordon had taken Dale Earnhardt Sr.'s place as the best driver in NASCAR. Many of Dale Earnhardt Sr.'s fans resented Gordon for that. They wanted someone to finally beat Gordon and saw Dale Jr. as their greatest hope. It was a lot to ask from a rookie.

SPEEDWEEK

Most sports have their most important event at the end of the season. For the National Football League (NFL), the season ends with the Super Bowl. For Major League Baseball, it's the World Series. But NASCAR's biggest race of the year is its first, the Daytona 500. The week leading up to the Daytona 500 is called Speedweek. Drivers make their qualifying runs a week before the race. But only the top two qualifiers earn their starting spots for the race. The rest of the drivers take part in special qualifying races to determine their starting position.

In February, Dale and his Winston Cup team went to Daytona to start the season. It was Dale's first Daytona 500. As a youngster, he'd always been in school when the big event took place, so he'd never been able to see the race in person.

The first step was to qualify for the race. Because Dale was a rookie, he wasn't guaranteed a spot in the field. He had to earn his spot during qualifying. If he did poorly, he'd be watching the race with the rest of his team.

The Daytona 500 has the most complex qualifying system of any race. Normal qualifying laps determine the pole position. But the rest of the spots are decided in a pair of fifty-lap qualifying races held in the week before the main event.

Dale had the twenty-second-best time in the qualifying laps. He'd have to finish fifteenth or better in his 125-mile qualifying race to make it into the big race.

When his qualifying race finally started, Dale was nervous. He didn't want to disappoint all of the fans who had come to see him drive. He was careful for the first few laps, not wanting to make a mistake. But soon he realized that he had a fast car. He began passing other cars. By the end of the race, he was in fourth place and had earned a spot in the main event. He shouted as his crew chief, Tony Eury, congratulated him over the radio.

When the driver positions were finally set, it turned out that Dale was the top-qualifying rookie. Kenseth would begin the race in twenty-fourth place.

LEAVING HIS MARK

Before the Daytona 500, Dale and his father both raced in an IROC race. At one point, they battled for the lead and Dale Jr. bumped his dad. After the race, Dale went to his father's car and found a bit of paint from his car that had scraped off during the bump. He circled the spot with a marker and wrote *Hi Dad! Dale Jr.* next to it.

Finally Sunday came, and Dale took his No. 8 Chevrolet onto the track. As the green flag dropped, he stomped on the accelerator and didn't let up. As with most races at Daytona, all forty-three cars in the field ran very close together. They had to stay close to keep in the draft. It's a winning strategy, but racing in such tight packs can also lead to multicar accidents.

Dale handled the pressure well and remained near the front for most of the day. After a caution flag on lap 156, Eury decided to change only two tires during Dale's pit stop. The short pit stop allowed Dale to leave pit row in second place. But it was also a risky move because most of the other cars got four fresh tires. Dale would need a lot of skill and a little luck to make the gamble work. Unfortunately, Dale didn't get the luck he needed. Nobody would help him draft. As soon as the green flag flew, he started losing positions. Even his dad wouldn't help him.

By the time it was over, Dale had fallen back to thirteenth place (Dale Sr. finished twenty-first, while Kenseth finished tenth). It was still a good finish for a rookie, but after coming out second from the last pit stop, Dale had hoped for better.

Dale's rookie season followed a similar pattern for the first few months. He often qualified well but had trouble holding on for good finishes.

He did score a top-ten finish in the third race of the year at Las Vegas, Nevada. After starting third, he pulled onto the track with the threat of rain. The drivers had to complete half of the scheduled laps for the race to be official. Dale jumped out to an early lead, but twenty laps into the race, the rain started to fall. NASCAR parked all of the cars to wait for the weather to improve. After the restart, Dale began falling back. He was in tenth place when the rain started again. The race was more than half finished, so NASCAR called the rest off.

By the beginning of April, Dale was feeling comfortable as a Winston Cup driver. He was ready for a big finish. The DIRECTV 500 at Texas Motor Speedway seemed like a good chance for Dale to take the next step. It was the same track where Dale had scored his first Busch Series win. Dale had a strong qualifying run with the fourth-fastest time.

Dale started the race carefully. In past races, he had raced too hard in the early laps and used up his tires. Worn tires don't give good grip. Without good grip, drivers have to slow down more in turns.

By lap one hundred, Dale and Matt Kenseth had moved to the front together. They both had great cars and were pulling away from the field. Seventy laps later, Kenseth got a penalty for a pit lane violation. Dale was out front by himself. Still, the race was less than half done.

Shortly after one of Dale's pit stops, an accident caused a caution. The timing was bad for Dale (as well as many other drivers) because two cars had not yet made pit stops. The caution flag froze the field and left Dale a full lap behind the cars that hadn't pitted. Those two cars got to pit under the caution flag and not lose a lap. With only one hundred laps left, Dale was still a lap down and he was getting impatient. Finally, another caution allowed Dale to get back on the lead lap. Dale took the lead back only fifteen laps later. He had a great final pit stop and won the race by more than six seconds over Jeff Burton.

Dale screamed over his radio as he completed the final turn and crossed the finish line. The crowd stood and cheered loudly. Thousands of flashes went off as people snapped photos of Dale's first Winston Cup win. After taking a victory lap, Dale pulled his car to Victory Lane to celebrate with his teammates.

As he stopped in the car, Dale Sr., who had finished seventh, stuck his head in the car's window to congratulate his son. Afterward Dale revealed his father's message to reporters, saying, "He just told me he loved me and he wanted to make sure I took time to enjoy this."

After only twelve Winston Cup starts, Dale was a winner. Only one NASCAR driver since 1950, Ron Bouchard, had won a race in fewer tries. Bouchard got his first victory in his eleventh start.

❝*I feel like a rock star every once in a while. It's kind of fun.*❞
—DALE EARNHARDT JR. ON BEING A CELEBRITY

Dale didn't need another twelve races to win again. Just four races later, he scored his second Winston Cup victory at the Pontiac Excitement 400 in Richmond, Virginia. After starting fifth for the Saturday night race, Dale found himself getting passed. He wasn't happy with the way his car was handling. His pit crew kept working on the car, though. Finally they fixed all of the problems and Dale started moving forward. When a caution came with 137 laps left, Eury decided not to make a pit stop. Dale stayed on the track. The decision moved him up to second place.

Tony Stewart was leading and appeared set to win the race. Dale feared that second place might be the best he could do. But as he pulled out of his pit stall on the final pit stop of the race, he ran into the left rear of Stewart's car. The contact gave Stewart a flat tire while Dale's car was unharmed. Stewart had to come back into the pits for a new tire, ending his chances to win.

When Dale returned to the track, he expected to be in the lead. But one car had changed only two tires during the pit stop. After being deep in the field for most of the day, Dale Earnhardt Sr. had surged ahead to the front. To win this race, Dale Jr. would have to pass his dad.

With Dale Jr. on four fresh tires, the race for the lead was no contest. Dale Jr. quickly blew by his dad. Terry Labonte also passed Dale Sr. and was quickly closing the gap between his car and Dale's. With two laps left, Labonte was right up to Dale's bumper. By the last lap, the cars were side by side. Dale held on tight and crossed the finish line 0.159 second before Labonte, becoming the first driver to win two races in 2000.

Dale's next win came at The Winston in Charlotte, North Carolina. The Winston isn't a regular Winston Cup race—it's NASCAR's all-star race. NASCAR invites twenty drivers who have either wins or championships to the race. Drivers don't earn points for their finishes, but they can still win big cash prizes. Before the race, some of Dale's teammates predicted that he would win. He didn't disappoint, despite hitting the outside wall hard about halfway through the race. Once again Dale celebrated with his teammates and his father. He dedicated the win to his friend and fellow driver Adam Petty, who had been killed in a crash earlier in the week.

Dale later said that the celebration was one of the happiest times of his life. "At that very moment, I felt like I would never enjoy another win as much as I enjoyed that feeling I was having. Dad and I . . . jumped around and hollered and made fools of ourselves on national television. It was a lot of fun."

IS THAT FOR ME?

As Dale celebrated his win at The Winston, he heard the crowd chanting "Earnhardt, Earnhardt!" He looked around for his father for a few moments until he realized that the people were cheering for him.

Dale followed up his win at The Winston by winning the pole for the Coca-Cola 600, where he finished fourth. He finished tenth the next week in Dover. But after that, his season quickly went downhill. While Dale struggled, Kenseth, who had won the Coca-Cola 600, charged into the lead in the Rookie of the Year standings.

After posting five top-ten finishes in the season's first thirteen races, Dale didn't have a single top-ten finish in the last twenty-one races. Every week Dale and his team seemed to find a new way to fail. At the year's first race at Pocono Raceway in Pennsylvania in June, an accident with his dad damaged Dale's car. At the second Pocono race in July, Dale ran out of gas. In July at Daytona, Dale ran into Jeff Gordon and damaged the car's radiator. At Watkins Glen, he slammed into a barrier and wrecked the car. Meanwhile, Kenseth continued to have good finishes. Dale's chance to win Rookie of the Year was slipping away.

One of the few highlights of the second half of Dale's season came at the Pepsi 400 in Michigan. Dale had a great qualifying run and won the pole. But that wasn't the reason the day was special. Dale's half brother, Kerry, also qualified for the race. It was Kerry's first Winston Cup race and the first time that a father and two of his sons drove in the same race since Lee Petty and his sons, Maurice and Richard, did it in the 1960s. Dale Jr. started first; Kerry started twenty-sixth; Dale Sr. started thirty-seventh.

The excitement of starting with his brother and dad quickly wore off. Kerry wrecked his car only fourteen laps into the race. Meanwhile, Dale fell back to thirty-fifth place. Then, with eleven laps left, his engine blew up. He pulled to the garage with a disappointing thirty-first-place finish. Dale Sr. had the only good finish of the three Earnhardts, crossing the line sixth.

Dale's bad luck continued. At Bristol, a gas called carbon monoxide built up inside his car and made him feel sick. At Darlington, Dale had a great car, but he made a pit stop shortly before rain ended the race and pinned him deep in the field. At New Hampshire, Dale had problems with his radio and smashed into the wall late in the race. At Martinsville, Dale crashed his car four times in one race. Dale called it the low point of his season.

The string of bad finishes frustrated Dale. In an online journal entry for NASCAR.com, he wrote: "I don't doubt my ability to be a winner, and until it happens again, I learn more about how to handle losing."

Still, the season wasn't over. In Charlotte NASCAR officials caught Dale speeding down pit row and made him serve a penalty. Dale had to sit still in his pit stall for fifteen seconds after his team finished work on the car. At Talladega Superspeedway in Alabama, he led the race with only a few laps left but almost spun on the last lap and finished fourteenth. In Rockingham, North Carolina, Dale again had a great car, but Kurt Busch ran into the back of his car and sent him crashing into the wall. In Phoenix, Arizona, Dale drove with a bad case of the flu. Finally, in the last race of the year in Atlanta, Georgia, Dale ran into John Andretti's car in the pits and limped to a twentieth-place finish.

Despite winning three races, Dale was disappointed with his rookie season. He finished sixteenth in the Winston Cup standings and lost the Rookie of the Year Award to Matt Kenseth. "My driving was not what it should have been, and our race cars weren't as good as they should have been, either," Dale later wrote of his disappointing second half.

TRACK RIVAL

Early in their careers, Dale and Matt Kenseth always seemed to be battling each other. They quickly developed a friendly rivalry. While they were friends off the track, they were fierce competitors on it. "As much as I like Matt and enjoy hanging with him, I really want to beat him," Dale said of his friend.

Still, Dale had given his fans a reason to be excited for 2001. He vowed to be a calmer and more consistent driver. Dale Earnhardt Sr. had finished the season in second place to Bobby Labonte for the Winston Cup title. Dale hoped that in 2001, his dad would finish second again—this time to his son.

Dale Earnhardt Jr. poses with his father, Dale Earnhardt Sr. *(center left)*, and his stepmother, Teresa Earnhardt *(far left)*, after the Hotwheels.com 300, the final race of the 1999 Busch Series season. Dale Jr.'s second-place finish at Homestead, Florida, helped him become Busch Series champion for the second year in a row.

During a race, Dale Jr. spends many hours strapped into his No. 8 car. The cockpit of his car may be as hot as 140 degrees Fahrenheit.

Speedy pit stops can make all the difference in a close race.

Dale Earnhardt Jr. picked up a lot of advice from his father *(left)* during the years they raced together.

© Brian Cleary/Icon SMI

© Reuters/CORBIS

Dale Jr. and his stepmother, Teresa, prepare to speak to reporters about Dale Sr.'s death on February 18, 2001, during the Daytona 500.

Dale Jr.'s No. 8 car creeps up behind Jeff Gordon's No. 24 car.

Dale Jr. walks away after a fiery crash during a practice session for a 2004 Le Mans Series race in Sonoma, California.

Autograph seekers and photographers surround Dale Jr. at a special Dale Earnhardt Jr. Day in Miami, Florida.

After winning the 2004 EA Sports 500 at Talladega, Dale Jr. and his team have a chance to celebrate.

Chapter | Seven

Tragedy

A month after the 2000 season ended, Dale had a dream about the 2001 Daytona 500. "I was out front all day. I kept telling myself I won it in my second time in the race," he recalled. But Dale's dream was a little odd—his father wasn't at the race. It seemed strange, but Dale didn't pay much attention to the dream at the time.

A week before the Daytona started the 2001 Winston Cup series, Dale got a chance to race on a team with his dad. Together with Andy Pilgram and Kerry Collins, father and son entered Daytona's Rolex 24 Hours race. In this endurance race, four drivers take turns driving a Corvette over an entire day. The team finished the race fourth.

Dale enjoyed the Rolex race, but as soon as it was done, his attention turned to the Daytona 500. He had high hopes for 2001, and he wanted to start the season off right.

In Dale's qualifying race, he and Mike Skinner had a photo finish, with Dale just barely losing. His finish earned him the sixth starting spot for the Daytona 500. Dale's success carried over to the main event, held on February 18. He stayed near the front for most of the race, along with his teammate, fellow DEI driver Michael Waltrip. Because Dale and Michael worked out of the same garage and had the same owner, they worked together on the track. But in the end, each driver was doing his best to win the race.

Late in the race, Tony Stewart was involved in a huge crash. His car sailed into the air and landed upside down on top of Bobby Labonte's car. It was a violent and spectacular wreck, but Stewart walked away. Many fans were amazed at how well protected NASCAR drivers were inside their cars.

After a long caution, the race restarted. On the final lap, Dale trailed only Waltrip. The teammates worked together, hoping to finish in the top two spots. Dale had no plans to pass Waltrip, who was going for his first Winston Cup win after years of trying. Behind Waltrip and Dale Jr. was Dale Sr., who was helping to keep all of the other cars from catching them.

As the leaders came around the final turn of the race, Dale Sr. was battling with Sterling Marlin for third place. Their cars made contact, causing Earnhardt's car to spin. Ken Schrader then ran into Earnhardt and they both smashed into the outside wall.

Meanwhile, Waltrip and Dale Jr. crossed the finish line. The crowd cheered Waltrip's first win, and at first, some people didn't even notice the crash that had demolished Dale Sr.'s car.

The two wrecked cars slid to a stop. Schrader quickly got out of his car. Dale Sr. did not. Schrader ran to Earnhardt's car to check on his friend. He looked inside, then frantically signaled for medical crews to come help.

The emergency crews rushed to the accident. As they arrived, the crowd, and Dale Jr., began to realize that something was seriously wrong. The medical crews pulled Dale Sr. from the car and took him by ambulance to a nearby hospital. Meanwhile, the crowd grew silent and the mood at the track was somber.

A TRIBUTE

In 2000, Dale Jr. wrote a tribute to his father. It read, in part: "This man could lead the world's finest army. He has wisdom that knows no bounds. No fire could burn his character, no stone could break it. . . . In every result, he stands as an example of what hard work and dedication will achieve. . . . I wonder what his future holds. To this point, he's only barely satisfied. His eyes see so much more than my imagination could produce. He is Dale Earnhardt."

A few hours later, NASCAR president Mike Helton spoke with reporters. "This is undoubtedly one of the most difficult announcements I've ever had to make," Helton said. "But after the accident in turn four of the Daytona 500, we've lost Dale Earnhardt." Bill France Jr., whose father started NASCAR, added, "Today, NASCAR lost its greatest driver in the history of the sport."

The news felt like a physical blow to Dale Jr. It hardly seemed real. He couldn't imagine not having his father there to talk to and celebrate with. He couldn't believe that his father wouldn't be there when he got married, when he had children. All his life, he'd lived in his father's shadow, and suddenly that shadow was gone. Dale felt very alone.

❝The weeks after Dad's death were a blur. I was surrounded by people all of the time, but it was like being on a raft in the ocean: surrounded by water but unable to drink any of it. I missed my dad every moment.❞

—DALE EARNHARDT JR.

On February 22, four days after Dale Sr.'s death, Dale Jr., his family, and thousands of friends, fellow drivers, and others touched by Dale Sr.'s life gathered for a memorial service in

Charlotte. Dale Sr. was so popular and the racing world was so sad at his passing that the service was broadcast on national television. There, Dale Jr. and the world tried to say good-bye to one of NASCAR's greatest champions.

Chapter | Eight

The Race Goes On

Dale and his DEI teammates quickly came to a decision about the next race and the rest of the NASCAR season. They would keep racing. Dale knew that his father would want him back in his car.

The next Sunday, Dale Jr. was out on the track, trying to put the Daytona tragedy behind him, just for a little while. But as hard as he tried, Dale couldn't get his mind on the race. On the first lap of the race, he crashed into the wall. Still, the day wasn't a total loss for DEI. Dale's teammate Steve Park won the race and showed that the team Dale Sr. had built was still strong. DEI had two wins in two races.

Dale continued to struggle, though. Not only did he miss his dad; he also had a lot more pressure on him. Dale Sr. had millions of fans, and after his death, many of them pinned their hopes on his son. Twenty-five-year-old Dale Jr. didn't respond well. He finished no better than fifteenth in the next four races.

The first race of April was at Texas Motor Speedway, where Dale had won his first Winston Cup race. It was there that Dale finally broke out of his bad streak. After winning the pole, Dale scored his first top-ten finish since his father's death. He followed that up by finishing in the top ten in four of his next six races. His early struggles had left him far behind in the Winston Cup standings, but his string of strong finishes gave him hope he could get back into the championship chase.

But Dale couldn't keep the momentum going. In the next three races, he finished thirty-ninth, nineteenth, and twentieth. Any hopes of a championship disappeared. By the season's halfway point, Dale was just hoping he would win a race.

❝*I had this little bit of a brat in me somewhere. That's all gone. The way I look at racing . . . the way I feel about going to the track . . . the way I prepare myself for each race is totally different.*❞

—DALE EARNHARDT JR., TALKING ABOUT
LIFE AFTER HIS FATHER'S DEATH.

On July 7, NASCAR returned to Daytona for the first time since Dale Sr.'s death. It was a strange time for Dale, but he was determined not to be afraid. He left for Daytona a day earlier than usual. He went onto the track and found the spot where his dad's accident had happened. The skid marks from the car's tires were still visible. Dale spent some time there, thinking about his dad.

Dale qualified for the thirteenth starting position. On Saturday evening, he pulled his Chevrolet onto the track and took a deep breath. The media and the fans had made a big deal about his return to Daytona, and he badly wanted a win. He wasn't alone. Dale's team and crew chief knew how important a win would be, both for Dale's fans and for his season. Tony Eury and his team worked hard to build the best car they could. They wanted to give Dale every chance to honor his father with a win.

Early on, it looked like he might get it. He led for many of the early laps and had one of the strongest cars on the track. "The car was a dream," Dale later wrote.

A caution flag flew late in the race, leaving Dale and Eury with a difficult decision. Should they change four tires or just two? They decided to get four new tires. The decision knocked them back to sixth place on the track. But the car was working well, and Dale believed he could march back to the front.

The strategy worked. Dale's car was better on four fresh tires than the cars ahead of him, which had only two new tires. He quickly worked his way back to the front. With only a few laps, Michael Waltrip was the only driver who could really challenge Dale for the lead. But Waltrip was Dale's teammate, and Dale had helped push Waltrip to a win at the Daytona 500 in February. He wasn't about to pass Dale and take away the win, so he just followed him across the finish line.

Dale was so happy and relieved that he needed a big celebration. He drove onto the grassy area on the inside of the frontstretch and did a burnout by stepping down hard on the accelerator and spinning his tires in the grass. He eventually found his way to Victory Lane, where his crew, teammates, and fellow drivers were all eager to congratulate him.

"That reminded me of someone I once knew," said longtime driver Dale Jarrett. Clearly Dale Jr. had picked up a few passing tricks from his father.

In 2002 Dale wrote a book, titled *Driver #8*, about his rookie season. In the best-selling book, he wrote about life on the Winston Cup circuit, his feelings about his disappointing season, his rivalry with Matt Kenseth, and his father's death.

Dale soaked in the moment, celebrating with friends, family, and teammates until morning. But his good feelings couldn't last forever. Soon after the race was done, some media members and even fellow drivers were asking questions about the win. They thought Dale's car had been just a bit too good. A few suggested that NASCAR had fixed the race so that Dale would win.

"I just couldn't believe it," Dale said of the idea. "I mean, aside from the days that I had my father with me, that was the greatest day of my life. I just can't believe people would step on me like that."

Dale won again two months later. Again his victory came in the face of a tragedy. On September 11, 2001, terrorists hijacked four airliners and attacked the World Trade Center in New York and the Pentagon in Washington, D.C. On September 23, NASCAR ran the first race after the attacks. Dale led 193 of 400 laps but found himself in third place after the final pit stop. He needed only twelve laps to pass Dale Jarrett and Jerry Nadeau, though, and he never looked back. After the race, Dale asked his team to bring him a U.S. flag he'd seen in the pit area. He held the flag out the window of his car and drove a victory lap.

"It does make me proud that I'm American," Dale said. "I feel honored that I was the one to win on a day like today. I mean, it didn't matter who won; it was healing to be here and it was special to be together and feel like the NASCAR family was together for the country."

A month later, Dale had a chance to prove that his win at Daytona hadn't been a fluke or a fix. The EA Sports 500 was held at Talladega, which is the only other track besides Daytona where NASCAR uses restrictor plates. After starting sixth, Dale stayed out front for most of the race and managed to stay out of a huge sixteen-car crash. Dale battled Tony Stewart on the last lap and won the race by only 0.388 second. The win, Dale's third of the year, moved him up to sixth in the Winston Cup standings. It also earned him the biggest payday of his racing career, a total of $1,165,773.

AUTOGRAPHS

Dale quickly learned that signing autographs is a big part of his job as a NASCAR star. His father had always signed his full name, but Dale wanted a signature that didn't take as long to write. He signs most of his autographs simply *Dale Jr.* He sometimes adds *#8* beneath the name.

The Talladega win was the last highlight of Dale's 2001 season, though. He scored only one top-ten finish in the final five races and dropped to eighth in the Winston Cup standings. It wasn't the way Dale wanted to finish, but he had shown that he could overcome adversity.

The year 2002 began as badly as 2001 had ended. After qualifying fifth for the Daytona 500, Dale finished a disappointing twenty-ninth. After finishes of twenty-sixth and sixteenth in the next two races, Dale was in twenty-fifth place in the Winston Cup standings. The season was quickly heading in the wrong direction.

Twenty-seven-year-old Dale didn't want to suffer through another losing season. He and his teammates were determined to turn things around. The change started at the MBNA America 500 in Atlanta. Dale had the second-best car on the track and he got everything he could out of it. His effort wasn't enough to beat Tony Stewart, though. Stewart dominated and Dale was never able to mount a serious charge in the race's final laps. Still, after the way the season had started, second place felt good for Dale and his teammates.

The Atlanta race started a hot streak. Dale finished in the top five in three of the next four races. Finally, at the Aaron's 499 in Talladega, Dale got his first win of the season. It was a familiar scene, reminding many fans of Dale's last win at the EA Sports 500 in Talladega. Again Earnhardt dominated and his teammate Michael Waltrip finished a close second. "When [Michael and I] work together like that, we're pretty hard to beat," Dale commented.

Dale had won three out of the last four restrictor-plate races. More important, he had moved up to fifth in the

Winston Cup standings. Suddenly Dale was a championship contender.

The next week at the NAPA Auto Parts 500 at California Speedway, all of that changed in an instant. With about twenty laps left in the race, Dale was running with the lead group. Next to him, Kevin Harvick blew a tire and lost control of his car, which swerved and tapped Dale's car. The contact sent Dale speeding into the outside wall at 130 miles per hour. It was a violent hit, but Dale managed to get out of the car and walk away. He had hit his head, had the wind knocked out of him, and hurt his ankle, but he insisted that he was all right.

"ANTI-POP"

Dale is a big music fan. One of his favorite groups is the Matthew Good Band. In 2002 he appeared in the group's video "Anti-Pop." In the video, Dale and lead singer Matthew Good steal a small gnome statue, then travel around North America taking photos of it in strange places.

Dale didn't tell anyone that his head hurt—a lot. He'd suffered a concussion, a bruise to the brain. He was having trouble thinking clearly, but he never told his team or NASCAR officials.

Dale feared that they'd make him sit out of some races. His teammate Steve Park had suffered a head injury in a 2001 wreck and after sitting out, Park was not as good a driver as he had been before the accident. Dale didn't want to suffer the same fate, so he lied about the extent of his injury.

"I didn't want to tell until it got better and I started to run better," Dale said. "Steve, he couldn't hide his injury and he dealt with so much [stuff] over it: 'He's never going to be the same, he's [messed] up, he's a write-off.' In the garage, all kinds of people have that idea, and I didn't want to go through that. So I didn't tell anybody."

For the next couple of months, Dale struggled just to concentrate. Some people noticed that his speech was slower than usual. He seemed to need an extra second or two to understand a new idea. Worst of all, his reactions on the track weren't what they should be. In the next seven races, he finished better than thirtieth only twice and never finished in the top ten. He later said that he didn't really feel back to normal until July. By that time, he had fallen to sixteenth in the Winston Cup standings.

Finally, at the Pepsi 400 in Daytona on July 6, Dale finished in the top ten. He did it again the next week at the Tropicana 400 in Chicago. But he didn't return to victory lane until he returned to Talladega in October.

Before the EA Sports 500, Dale had a feeling fuel mileage might play a big part in the race. NASCAR had just made a new rule to make fuel cells smaller at restrictor-plate tracks. The idea behind the rule was to make teams pit more often and prevent cars from running in huge—and dangerous—packs. Dale sat down to figure out exactly how far he could go on one tank of gas. He decided that his car could go thirty-eight laps and not a bit more.

After starting thirteenth, Dale showed that he had a strong car, working his way to the front. But he still needed a little luck to win. A caution flag flew late in the race, setting up his final pit stop with exactly thirty-eight laps left. He knew he should be able to finish without another stop. Dale's calculations were perfect. He had just enough fuel to cross the finish line in first place. He ran out of fuel on the way to Victory Lane.

"I ain't really doing much, just turning left every once in a while," Dale said after the race. "That car's got to go and the Bud team makes it go. We already had good gas mileage, but I lifted [off the gas pedal] a lot, especially the last half of the race."

The win helped the team finish the season strong. Dale scored top-ten finishes in six of the final eight races and ended the season in eleventh place, three spots behind his 2001 finish.

Dale was tired of losing. He was ready to give his team the consistency needed to win a title. Once again, he vowed to be a contender next year.

Chapter Nine

An Old Rivalry

Dale's career continued to mirror that of his friend and rival Matt Kenseth. In 2002 Kenseth won more races— five—than any other Winston Cup driver. But like Dale, Kenseth was having trouble with consistency. Despite all of his wins, Kenseth had finished a distant eighth in the 2002 Cup standings. The two drivers who had battled for two Busch Series titles and the Winston Cup Rookie of the Year each needed to learn how to finish well every week. In 2003 their careers crossed paths again as they both learned their lessons and battled for the Winston Cup title.

At first Dale's team didn't look like it had learned much of anything. After qualifying second for the Daytona 500, the team had a battery problem that caused Dale to lose three laps in the pits. The mistake left the team with a disappointing thirty-sixth-place finish. Dale's performance didn't get any better the next week in Rockingham, where he finished thirty-third. Much like they had in 2002, Dale and his teammates dug a deep hole early in the season. After two races, they stood in thirty-eighth place in the Winston Cup standings. It was no way to start a title chase.

Dale didn't let the failures get him down. A second-place finish at the UAW-Daimler Chrysler 400 in Las Vegas sparked a streak of great racing. The team finished in the top ten in seven of the next eight races.

66*You never really can put a price on having great people around you. We've got key people in great positions.*99

—DALE EARNHARDT JR. ON HIS CREW

One of those races was the Aaron's 499 at Talladega, the track where Dale's last three wins had come. If Dale could win this race, he'd become the first driver since Bill Elliot in 1985 and 1986 to win four straight races at one track. A win would also make him the second-most successful driver in Talladega history. Only one man—Dale Earnhardt Sr.—had won more than four races there.

Early in the race, Dale was involved in a huge twenty-seven-car crash. But he had only light damage, and his team used several yellow-flag pit stops to fix the car. Once the car was fixed, Dale was on the move. On lap 185, he made a controversial pass of Kenseth that appeared to be from below the yellow line on the inside part of the track. NASCAR rules state that a driver cannot make a pass from below the yellow line. But NASCAR officials decided that Dale had already made the pass before he went below the line. Many people disagreed with the decision, but Dale wasn't about to argue. The pass helped to send him to the front and to his fourth-straight Talladega win.

Dale's goal of having consistent finishes was becoming a reality. The Talladega win moved him to second place in the Winston Cup standings, 129 points behind Kenseth.

On May 3, Dale finished in third place at the Pontiac Excitement 400 in Richmond. The finish pulled him to within a mere 20 points of Kenseth, a difference of only a few spots on the track. He hoped to jump into the lead the next week at the Coca-Cola 600, but brake problems left him in forty-first place. It was his only really bad finish of the spring and summer. Try as he might, Dale just could not catch Kenseth.

While many racing fans and experts thought Dale's consistent driving showed that he had matured, others criticized him. Although he was getting plenty of top-five finishes, Dale wasn't winning. He hadn't won a race at a track other than Talladega in almost two years. Only three of his eight career Winston Cup wins had come in non-restrictor-plate races. Some people said this was proof that the team's cars, not its driver, were the real reason for Dale's success. After all, if Dale was such a great driver, why wasn't he winning at other tracks?

66NASCAR has always expected a lot from the guys who run up front and who are the most popular with fans, and it's important for us to hold up our end of the deal. For me, I have a chance to do some things and reach some people that the sport hasn't gotten to before.99

—DALE EARNHARDT JR.

The criticism didn't bother Dale much. As the summer turned into fall, he continued finishing well. He worked hard to keep up with Kenseth in the cup standings, spending most of the summer in second place, about 200 points out of the lead.

No matter what he did, Dale couldn't seem to gain ground. When he finished fourth at the Pocono 500, Kenseth finished third. When he finished seventh at the Sirius 400, Kenseth finished fourth. When he finished sixth at the New England 300, Kenseth was third. Dale and his teammates were thrilled to be getting such good finishes, but it was frustrating when they fell farther behind even on their good days. By the middle of September, Dale found himself more than 400 points out of first place. Suddenly he knew how Kenseth must have felt trying to chase down Dale for the Busch Series championship several years before.

Still, Dale and his crew had hope. On September 28, the team was in Talladega for the EA Sports 500. It was by far Dale's best track, and he was going for a fifth-straight win there.

After qualifying thirty-eighth for the race, Dale knew he had his work cut out for him. He didn't dominate the race as he often did, but he stayed near the front for most of the day. With about thirty laps left, Dale got some good news—Kenseth's engine had blown up. Dale finally had a chance to gain some ground in the standings. He charged to the front and took the lead with about twenty laps left. But a lap later, Jeff Burton also blew an engine, causing a caution. Like most drivers, Dale came in for a pit stop. But it wasn't the Bud team's best stop—two cars passed Dale in the pits.

When the race restarted, the battle for the lead was fierce. Nobody was willing to settle for second place. With only a few laps left, Waltrip took the lead. Dale followed his teammate for the next few laps. On the last lap, Dale drove right up to Waltrip's bumper, but he couldn't pass. He finished second, barely missing his chance at a fifth-straight Talladega win. The team was disappointed that they didn't get their second win of the year, but it was still a good day. DEI cars had finished first and second, and Dale had gained a lot of points in the Winston Cup standings.

In 2003 Dale was voted NASCAR's Most Popular Driver. He received more fan votes than the next ten drivers combined.

Kenseth's bad luck at Talladega was exactly what Dale needed if he was going to win the championship. But one blown engine wasn't enough. Only seven races remained, and Dale was still more than 300 points behind. Kenseth would need to have at least three more bad finishes for Dale to have a shot.

Meanwhile, Dale did everything he could to make up points. He finished in the top ten in four of the next five races. The last of those five races was the Checker Auto Parts 500 in Phoenix. Dale entered the race 258 points behind Kenseth with three races to go. He needed to win, something he hadn't done at a non-restrictor-plate track in more than two years.

Both Dale and Kenseth ran in the top ten for most of the race, but Dale's car was a bit stronger. With about one hundred laps left, Dale came in for his final pit stop. He and Tony Eury agreed to change four tires. Dale wanted the best-possible grip for the last segment of the race. The decision paid off. Dale's car was very fast on the fresh tires. With about fifty laps left, he passed Jimmie Johnson for the lead. Despite a few caution flags that caused restarts, Dale never gave up his lead. Finally, he'd won on a track other than Talladega. He was happy for that streak to be over.

"It was great to see the expression of the guys when I came to Victory Lane," Dale said. "They've put their heart and soul into trying to make this team better."

 Dale's favorite sports team is a football team—the Washington Redskins.

The win was great for Dale and his team, but it didn't gain him much in the cup standings. Kenseth finished the race sixth, and with two races left, his lead over Dale stood at 228 points. For Dale to have a shot at the title, Kenseth would need at least one, and probably two, bad finishes in those races.

Kenseth didn't give Dale that shot. He finished fourth the next week at Rockingham, clinching the NASCAR title. It was a good thing for Kenseth that he clinched the title a week early because he finished in last place in the season's final race.

Dale, meanwhile, finished thirteenth and twenty-fourth in the season's final two races, allowing Jimmie Johnson to overtake him for second place in the final standings. Dale finished the year in third place, 207 points behind Kenseth and 117 points behind Johnson. It was by far Dale's most successful Winston Cup season, but he wanted more.

Dale's confidence was high. He told reporters that if he could keep his team intact, he would win the championship in 2004.

Chapter Ten

The Chase

The year 2004 was a season of change for NASCAR. Its longtime sponsor decided not to renew its contract. For the first time in decades, the top stock car series would not be called the Winston Cup. Instead, it became the Nextel Cup.

The name wasn't the only change. Many fans and drivers had been upset about how Kenseth won the 2003 championship. Kenseth had won only a single race all year. NASCAR also didn't like how Kenseth's huge lead late in the season caused fans to lose interest in the sport. Because most NASCAR races are held on Sunday afternoons, races late in the season have to compete with NFL football games for television audiences. NASCAR wanted to be sure the end of the season was filled with excitement and drama.

NASCAR's solution was to add a new twist to the end of the season. The first twenty-six races of the thirty-six-race season would be kind of like a regular season. The top-ten drivers (as well as anyone else within 400 points of the leader) would be eligible for the "Chase for the Cup," a ten-race shoot-out for the title (each race still includes forty-three drivers, but only those who have qualified for the Chase are eligible to win the championship). After twenty-six races, NASCAR would erase the point totals for the drivers in the Chase. The driver who had led the standings after twenty-six races would start with 5,050 points. The second-place driver would start with 5,045 points and so on down the line. NASCAR officials hoped this would add a new element of excitement to the last part of the racing season.

Dale was eager to start the new season. He believed that his team was the favorite to win the title. During the first week of the season at Daytona, Dale proved that he meant business. He started the week by winning one of the 125-mile qualifying races. On Sunday, he won his first Daytona 500. Then on Monday, he returned to the track and won the rain-delayed Busch Series race. It was a dominating performance. Suddenly everyone wondered if Dale might be able to back up his big talk.

Dale and his team knew that consistency was the most important factor during the first twenty-six races of the year. A fifth-place finish in the season's second race, the Subway 400, gave the team a great start to the year. The team was in first place in the Nextel Cup standings, seven points ahead of

Kenseth. But in the next race in Las Vegas, Dale's car was terrible. He couldn't steer it in the turns and quickly fell four laps behind the leader. He ended the race in thirty-fifth place. The bad finish caused Dale to plummet to seventh in the standings, 125 points behind Kenseth, who'd won two races in a row.

VIDEO GAME STAR

Playing video games is one of Dale's hobbies. But he doesn't play only for fun—he also uses racing games to practice driving. In 2004 Dale and teammate Martin Truex Jr. used a strategy they had practiced in a video game during a real race at Talladega. In the game, they had learned to run along a higher part of the track than most cars run. The strategy worked in the game and it worked on the track, helping Truex to a win.

Despite the bad day, Dale still felt good about his position. With a few more good races, the team would be right back at the top. Dale didn't waste any time showing that the team was able to rebound from a bad week. In the season's fourth race, the Golden Corral 500 in Atlanta, Dale qualified seventh and quickly worked his way toward the front. With fifteen laps left in the race, he blew past Jeremy Mayfield and cruised to his second win of the season. More important, he moved back into the top five in the standings, right where he wanted to be.

"Last week was as bad as it ever gets," he said after the win. "But we didn't get on each other too bad, and we stayed pretty focused."

In the next month, he and his team proved that they were ready to be consistent, finishing in the top ten in four of the next five races. The good stretch of racing moved Dale back to the top of the Nextel Cup standings.

Dale's next win came on May 15 in Richmond. After starting the race fourth, he and several other drivers, including Tony Stewart, Bobby Labonte, and Jimmie Johnson, traded the lead all day long. Finally, with fifty-four laps left, a caution flag flew. Dale talked to Tony Eury on the radio. Eury thought that the car had enough fuel to finish the race. The team decided not to make a pit stop. Although new tires would make Dale faster, the time he would lose in the pits would drop him too far back in the field.

The strategy worked. Dale stayed out front, along with Jimmie Johnson, who also decided not to pit. The two drivers battled down the stretch, but Dale's car was just a little better. He held on to win his third race of the year. The win increased his lead in the standings to 40 points over Johnson. "I don't know if we had the best car tonight. Being out front at the end was where you needed to be," Dale told reporters. "So that's what we did."

Dale and his team kept on producing strong finishes. By the time the regular season was half over, Dale had built a 98-point lead over Johnson and a 179-point lead over Kenseth. His spot in the Chase for the Cup seemed almost assured. Only a real disaster could threaten his place among the top-ten drivers for the regular season.

On Sunday, July 18, a rare weekend without a Nextel Cup race, that disaster came. Because Dale didn't have a NASCAR race to run that weekend, he went to Infineon Raceway in Sonoma, California, to compete in an American Le Mans series race. Dale wasn't a part of the Le Mans series, but he thought he'd have fun trying one race.

66*He's very, very grounded, and it would amaze people what he thinks is important. It's friends, family, being at home. Those things are what's important to him, and in this life he has of traveling so much, I really don't see that changing.*99

—BRENDA JACKSON, DALE JR.'S MOTHER

On the day of the race, Dale and the other drivers took part in a short morning practice. Dale was driving his Corvette

C5-R, testing the twists and turns of the road course. In one of the turns, Dale lost control. The car slid and spun into a concrete barrier. The impact broke part of the car's fuel line. Instantly the car erupted in flames. Dale was still strapped tightly into his seat. The flames were around his legs and the car was quickly filling with smoke. Somehow Dale managed to unhook his restraints and crawl out of the Corvette. Safety crews hurried onto the track to put out the fire. Dale was rushed to a hospital.

"All I saw was fire," Dale said. "I didn't even see where to go to get out. I just got out somehow. But there was fire within the helmet and all around the visor. . . . I was just trying to find out how to get to where the fire wasn't."

Dale was treated for serious burns on his legs and chin. He was released from the hospital the next day. The good news was that none of his injuries was severe. But the bad news was that he was in a great deal of pain. He couldn't sit comfortably in his car. At first, his team thought he would have to miss the next race. Missing a whole race would be a huge blow to the team's championship hopes.

As the week went on, Dale made a decision. NASCAR rules state that the driver who starts a Nextel Cup race gets credit for all of the points in the race. Dale would still earn all of the points for his car's finish even if another driver finished the race for him. Despite his pain, Dale was going to start the next race, the Siemens 300 at New Hampshire International Speedway. The team planned for Martin Truex Jr. to take over once the first caution flag flew.

When Dale finally climbed into his car before the race, he was hoping for an early caution flag. He was in a lot of pain. To make the situation worse, his car wasn't handling well. The drivers completed lap after lap without a caution flag. Soon Dale fell a lap down. Finally, on lap sixty-one, the yellow flag flew. Dale pulled into his pit stop and got out of the car. The day ended with a thirty-first-place finish. It wasn't great, but it could have been a lot worse.

"My injuries really, really hurt bad," Dale said after he got out of the car. "It's a pain I've never felt before. But I was in two burn centers and I saw some people in there that were a lot worse off than I was and it made me really appreciate how lucky I was to be able to get out of there."

Dale wasn't ready for a full race the next week. Fifty-three laps into the Pennsylvania 500, he got out of his car and let John Andretti take over for him. The team finished twenty-fifth and Dale dropped to third in the standings, more than 200 points behind Jimmie Johnson.

On August 8, Dale was finally able to complete a race. Although he started well in the Brickyard 400 in Indianapolis, a flat tire late in the race dropped him to twenty-ninth place. It wasn't the finish he wanted, but Dale was back in his car for good. The team had survived his accident and his spot in the Chase for the Cup was still secure.

Most fans think of Dale as a superspeedway driver. He dominates big tracks like Daytona and Talladega. But after starting thirtieth in the Sharpie 500, held at the small, half-mile Bristol Motor Speedway, Dale reminded everyone that he could drive anywhere. Early in the race, Dale and Eury decided not to pit under a yellow flag, moving Dale to the front of the pack. From there, Dale went on to lead 295 of the race's 500 laps. It was one of his most dominant wins of the season.

Dale shouted with joy in Victory Lane. "This team is tough as nails! Man, we needed this. This is one of the biggest wins of my career. . . . You can't be number one all the time. That's what makes it sweeter."

The Bristol win, along with a second-place finish at Richmond two weeks later, helped Dale hold on to third place as the Nextel Cup's regular season ended. Dale entered the final race of the regular season more than 100 points out of first place, but none of that mattered once the Chase began. Under NASCAR's new scoring system, Dale was suddenly only 10 points behind leader Jeff Gordon. It was time for Dale to step up his efforts.

66Everybody is always telling me about my position in the sport and how far I reach and my impact here and there. I can't grasp it. That's one thing I wish I knew everything about. I don't know what my influence is. I don't know if I walk into a room, who is listening and who isn't.99

—DALE EARNHARDT JR.

The first race of the Chase was the Sylvania 300 at New Hampshire. Dale was leading the race about halfway through, but couldn't stay out front. He finished third and ended the day tied with race winner Kurt Busch atop the Chase standings.

"I was real worried about starting off the Chase with a poor finish," Dale said. "You can't take risks or wreck it, and you can't get involved in crashes or cut tires. . . . You're going to be a lot more nervous, I think, now than you were before every lap."

Dale knew that in a ten-race shoot-out, he couldn't afford bad finishes. He needed to make every race count. Over the first half of the Chase, Dale and his team showed the consistency they would need to win the title, finishing in the top ten in every race.

While Dale was driving like a champion on the track, he did hurt the team's chances off the track. After he won the EA Sports 500 at Talladega, Dale got out of his car in Victory Lane to celebrate. NBC, which broadcast the race, sent a reporter to interview Dale. During the interview, which was televised live, Dale cursed. Earlier in the year, NASCAR officials had warned drivers not to swear on television. NASCAR had already given several drivers fines and had docked them points for breaking the rule.

Two days after the incident, NASCAR officials handed down Dale's punishment. They fined him $10,000 and docked the team 25 points. The penalty knocked Dale out of the lead in the Chase standings. It was a big mistake that cost the team valuable points. Dale couldn't afford any more slipups.

Despite the mistake, Dale finished the first half of the Chase in second place, only 24 points behind Kurt Busch. If he could continue to put up strong finishes, the title would be his. But in the sixth race of the Chase, the Subway 500 at Martinsville, gear problems caused Dale to finish thirty-third. The next week in Atlanta, the team appeared to be on its way to bouncing back from the bad finish. But with fifteen laps left, Dale made a mistake and drove up into Carl Edwards while trying to pass for third place. What had looked like a good finish became another thirty-third-place disappointment. Suddenly Dale had fallen to fifth place in the standings, 98 points behind Busch. He needed a big finish.

Dale began his comeback at the Checker Auto Parts 500 in Phoenix. After starting fourteenth, Dale cruised toward the front. With ten laps left, he was in second place behind Jeff Gordon. But Dale's car was stronger and he had no trouble making the last pass.

"I knew we were a sitting duck," Gordon said. "The eight car was just so strong."

Dale was happy about his sixth win of the year, but his mind was still on the championship standings. The win put him in third place, 47 points behind Busch with two races left. "We don't feel any pressure," he said. "All we can do now is race."

In 2004 NASCAR announced it was planning to require the Steel and Foam Energy Reduction Barrier (SAFER) at all tracks for the 2005 season. The softer barriers were expected to protect drivers by absorbing more of a car's energy when the car slams into the wall surrounding the track.

Dale didn't have a bad day at the Southern 500, finishing eleventh. But all of the other drivers at the top of the Chase standings finished ahead of him. With only one race left, Dale found himself in fourth place, 72 points out of the lead. He would need to win the final race, the Ford 400 in Miami, and he would also need all of the other leaders to have problems.

Dale didn't get his way. Busch, Johnson, and Gordon battled one another at the front of the field in the closest NASCAR title finish ever. Busch ended up winning by 8 points over Johnson and 16 points over Gordon. Dale's twenty-third-place finish, meanwhile, dropped him to fifth place, 138 points out of the lead. Again Dale had come up short in his quest for a title. It was a disappointing end to a great season.

"Our expectations coming into this race were just to have fun, because we pretty much knew [winning the championship] was a long shot," Dale said. "I'm proud of my team. We had good days, and we had bad days, but we battled and put together our best season ever."

Always a Driver

Dale won six races in 2004, more than any other driver. He proved that he could win at short tracks as well as super-speedways. He and his teammates also showed that they could post the consistent finishes a champion needs. He remains one of the top drivers in NASCAR, and many experts feel it's only a matter of time before he earns his first Nextel Cup title.

Still, Dale wasn't content to just try again in 2005. He wanted to make some changes. Tony Eury left his job as Dale's crew chief. Pete Rondeau, Michael Waltrip's former crew chief, took over. Dale even wanted to change the cars. He gave Waltrip's team many of his cars and asked his team to start over.

At first Dale's changes looked like a disaster. The new crew brought a brand-new car to test at Daytona. The car was slow and it couldn't keep up with the other cars. By the time Speedweek came in February 2005, many fans were questioning whether Dale's team would continue to dominate at restrictor-plate tracks. After a bad qualifying run, even more people were wondering.

When the Daytona 500 finally started, Dale struggled. He was in the middle of the pack for most of the day. But as the race went on, he slowly started to move toward the front. Finally, in the last ten laps, he was battling with Tony Stewart, Jeff Gordon, and Kurt Busch for the lead. The Daytona crowd roared as Dale went to the outside of the track and shot past Stewart for the lead. But he couldn't hold on. With three laps left, Jeff Gordon used an outside move of his own to get past Dale just before a caution flag. On the restart, Dale couldn't catch Gordon. He finished third. It wasn't a win, but Dale's comeback showed that his new cars and his new team have what it takes to compete for a championship.

Dale's life is centered around racing. He lives in Mooresville, North Carolina, where he's always close to the action at DEI. Teresa Earnhardt runs DEI, and she is a regular at NASCAR races, where she cheers on Dale and the other DEI drivers.

Dale spends most of his time working with his team to make sure everything and everybody are ready for the next race. When he's not focused on the Nextel Cup, he enjoys driving in other kinds of races, like the Le Mans series. Even when he's at home, he's usually racing. He spends hours playing racing video games and even had a go-kart track built in his backyard. He often spends his free time with fellow drivers Jamie McMurray, Elliot Sadler, and, of course, his brother, Kerry.

Although he dates and has had several girlfriends, Dale says that he's not ready to get married and start a family. For now, Dale is content to focus on racing and on building the sport that his legendary father lived and died for.

PERSONAL STATISTICS

Name:

Ralph Dale Earnhardt Jr.

Nicknames:

Junior, Little E, Junebug

Born:

October 10, 1974

Height:

6'0"

Weight:

170 lbs.

Residence:

Mooresville, North Carolina

CAREER WINSTON CUP/NEXTEL CUP STATISTICS

YEAR	STARTS	WINS	TOP 5	TOP 10	WINNINGS
1999	5	0	0	1	$162,095
2000	34	2	3	10	$2,583,075
2001	36	3	9	15	$5,827,542
2002	36	2	11	16	$4,970,034
2003	36	2	13	21	$6,880,807
2004	36	6	16	21	$7,069,198
Career	183	15	52	84	$27,492,751

GLOSSARY

black flag: a flag waved to signal a penalty for a driver

caution: a race condition during which the track is unsafe for racing speeds. Wrecks, debris on the track, and rain can all bring out caution flags. During a caution, cars follow behind a pace car at a safe speed, usually 55 miles per hour. During a caution, cars on the track may not pass one another.

checkered flag: a flag waved to signal the end of the race

crew chief: the member of a racing team who manages the rest of the crew and makes strategy decisions during a race

drafting: a strategy in which a driver closely follows another driver to reduce wind resistance

green flag: a flag waved to start a race and to restart a race after a caution

pit stop: a stop during a race. The pit crew changes a car's tires, adds fuel, and makes fast repairs.

red flag: a flag waved to stop all of the cars—the track is unsafe to drive

restrictor plate: a metal plate that partially blocks the flow of air into an engine

road course: a track that includes many turns, both left and right. Some road courses even have hills.

rookie: a first-year driver

sponsor: a company that pays to advertise on a team's car

superspeedway: a very large oval track with banked turns

white flag: a flag waved to signal the final lap

yellow flag: a flag waved to signal a caution to drivers

SOURCES

3 Godwin Kelly, "Junior Up On High! Wins First Daytona 500," *www .news-journalonline.com*, February 15, 2004, http://www.news-journalonline.com/speed/daytona500/2004/03SpeedNEXT01021604.htm (April 14, 2005).

3 Ibid.

4 "Dale Earnhardt Jr. Wins Daytona 500," *Daytona International Speedway.com*, February 15, 2004, http://www .daytonainternationalspeedway .com/news/news.jsp?news_id=225 (April 14, 2005).

8 Kathy Persinger, *Dale Earnhardt Jr.: Born to Race* (Champaign, IL: Sports Publishing, 2001), 22.

8–9 Larry Cothren, *Earnhardt: A Racing Family Legacy* (St. Paul, MN: Motorbooks Publishing Company, 2003), 197.

10 Ibid., 199.

11 Ryan McGee, "Rising Son," *American Thunder*, March 2004, 50.

13 Cothren, *Earnhardt*, 201.

16 Ibid., 212.

18 Persinger, *Dale Earnhardt Jr.*, 30.

19 Cothren, *Earnhardt*, 244.

23 Ibid.

25 Ibid., 221.

25 "Busch Race Results," *tricklefan .com*, n.d., http://www.tricklefan .com/racin1998/news981.html (April 14, 2005).

26 Scott Butterworth, "Spencer Stays Strong to Edge Earnhardt Jr." *Review-Journal.com,* March 1, 1998, http://www.reviewjournal.com /lvrj_home/1998/Mar-01-Sun-1998 /sports/7050695.html (April 14, 2005).

28 Cothren, *Earnhardt*, 238.

28 Ibid., 220.

31 Associated Press, "Earnhardt Jr. Wins Busch Race," *Review-Journal.com*, July 6, 1998, http://www.reviewjournal.com/lvrj_home/1998/Jul-06-Mon-1998/

sports/7798541.html (April 14, 2005).

32 "NASCAR – Earnhardt Jr. Wins Busch Race," *RaceLink.com*, July 20, 1998, http://www.racelink .com/rl_news/archive/0798/drn _week4.html (April 14, 2005). "

33 Cothren, *Earnardt*, 246.

34 Ibid., 220.

35 Persinger, *Dale Earnhardt Jr.*, 42.

36 Ibid.

36–37 Ibid., 43.

39 David Poole, *Little E's Big Win* (Chicago: Triumph Books, 2004), 55

40 Cothren, *Earnhardt*, 256.

42 Persinger, *Dale Earnhardt Jr.*, 54.

43 Ryan McGee, "Rising Son," *American Thunder*, March 2004, 48.

44 Poole, *Little E's Big Win*, 59.

45 "10th NASCAR Busch Win!" *dalejrpitstop.com*, n.d., http:// www.dalejrpitstop.com/wins/ win-10.html (April 14, 2005).

46 "12th NASCAR Busch Win!" *dalejrpitstop.com*, n.d., http:// www.dalejrpitstop.com/wins/ win-12.html (April 14, 2005).

47–48 Cothren, Earnhardt, 250.

53 David Poole "Dale Jr. Says It All in the Victory Lap," *ThatsRacin.com*, April 2, 2000, http://www .thatsracin.com/mld/thatsracin/ archives/2756432.htm (April 14, 2005).

53 Cothren, *Earnhardt*, 250.

55 Poole, *Little E's Big Win*, 62.

57 Dale Earnhardt Jr. and Jade Gurss, *Driver #8* (New York: Warner Books, 2002), 248.

58 Earnhardt Jr., *Driver #8*, 342.

58 Ibid., 9.

59 Poole, *Little E's Big Win*, 66.

61 Earnhardt, *Driver #8*, 312–313.

62 Persinger, *Dale Earnhardt Jr.*, 78.

62 Ibid.

62 Earnhardt, *Driver #8*, 350.

65 Poole, *Little E's Big Win*, 75.

66 Earnhardt, *Driver #8,* 353.

67 Ibid., 354.

68 Poole, *Little E's Big Win*, 75.

68 "Dominant Day for Dale at Dover Downs," *dalejrpitstop.com*, n.d., http://www.dalejrpitstop.com/budpr/2001budpr-dov2-post.html (April 14, 2005).

70 Poole, *Little E's Big Win*, 32.

72 Chris Jenkins, "Earnhardt Jr. Says He Hid Concussion," *usatoday.com*, September 25, 2002, http://www.usatoday.com/sports/motor/nascar/2002-09-25-earnhardt-concussion_x.htm (April 14, 2005).

73 Marty Smith, "Dale Jr. Completes Sweep at Talladega," *NASCAR.com*, October 7, 2002, http://www.nascar.com/2002/news/headlines/wc/10/06/easports_500/index.html (April 14, 2005).

75 "Q & A with Dale Earnhardt Jr.," *CircleTrack.com*, n.d., http://www.circletrack.com/thehistoryof/36141/ (April 14, 2005).

77 Ryan McGee, "Rising Son," *American Thunder*, March 2004, 48.

80 Poole, *Little E's Big Win*, 39.

85 "Junior Marches into Georgia," *NASCAR.com*, March 15, 2004, http://www.nascar.com/races/cup/2004/4/index.html (April 14, 2005).

85–86 "Earnhardt Jr. Stays Out, Wins Easily at Richmond," *NASCAR.com*, May 16, 2004, http://www.nascar.com/2004/news/headlines/cup/05/15/bc.car..nascar.richmond.ap/index.html (April 14, 2005).

86 Skip Wood, "Dale Earnhardt Jr. Makes Mom Proud," *Tennessean.com*, May 8, 2000, http://www.tennessean.com/sii/00/05/08/race08.shtml (April 14, 2005).

87 Rupen Fofaria, "Just Starting Race No Minor Feat," *ESPN.com*, July 24, 2004, http://sports.espn.go.com/rpm/news/story?id=1845773 (April 14, 2005).

88 Lee Spencer, "Dale Jr.: 'Ain't Good Enough to Drive a Car'," *MSN.FoxSports.com*, n.d., http://msn.foxsports.com/story/2604518 (April 14, 2005).

89 "Earnhardt Ends Lengthy Slump With Bristol Win," *SI.com*, August 29, 2004, http://sportsillustrated.cnn.com/2004/racing/08/29/bc.car.nascar.bristol.ap/ (April 14, 2005).

90 Mark Ashenfeller, "Earnhardt Jr. Wiser, Seeking Respect," *ESPN.com*, October 6, 2004, http://sports.espn.go.com/rpm/news/story?id=1896397 (April 14, 2005).

90 Jerry Bonkowski, "Junior's Pace," *Yahoo! Sports*, September 20, 2004, http://ca.sports.yahoo.com/nascar/news?slug=jb-juniorloudon&prov=yhoo&type=lgns (April 14, 2005).

92 David Poole, "Dale Earnhardt Jr. Gets the Win at Phoenix: Points Race Tightens a Little More," *ThatsRacin.com*, November 7, 2004, http://www.thatsracin.com/mld/thatsracin/10123887.htm (April 14, 2005).

92 Ibid.

93 Marty Smith, "In Review: Earnhardt Jr.: NASCAR's Most Popular Driver Experienced a Bit of Everything in '04," *NASCAR.com*, December 19, 2004, http://www.nascar.com/2004/news/headlines/cup/12/19/dearnhardtjr_yir/index.html (April 14, 2005).

BIBLIOGRAPHY

Cothren, Larry. *Earnhardt: A Racing Family Legacy.* St. Paul, MN: Motorbooks Publishing Company, 2003.

Earnhardt, Dale Jr., and Jade Gurss. *Driver #8.* New York: Warner Vision Books, 2002.

Persinger, Kathy. *Dale Earnhardt Jr.: Born to Race.* Champaign, IL: Sports Publishing, 2001.

Poole, David. *Little E's Big Win.* Chicago: Triumph Books, 2004.

WEBSITES

NASCAR.com

http://nascar.com

The official site of NASCAR has feature articles, statistics, news updates, and racing schedules.

The Official Site of Dale Earnhardt Jr.

http://www.dalejr.com

Dale Jr.'s official Web page includes the latest news, upcoming events and appearances, statistics, and fan club information.

The Dale Earnhardt Jr. Pit Stop

http://www.dalejrpitstop.com

This fan site has photos, race reviews and quotes, statistics, and a Dale Earnhardt Jr. biography.

ESPN Motorsports

http://sports.espn.go.com/rpm/index

ESPN.com's section on motor sports includes the latest news in all forms of racing, including NASCAR.

INDEX

105